WORKING FOR VICTORY?

WORKING FOR VICTORY?

Images of women in the First World War, 1914–18

Diana Condell and Jean Liddiard

ROUTLEDGE & KEGAN PAUL
London

First published in 1987 by
Routledge & Kegan Paul Ltd
11 New Fetter Lane, London EC4P 4EE

Set in Photina
Printed in Great Britain by
Butler & Tanner Ltd, Frome and London

British Library Cataloguing in Publication Data

Working for victory?: images of women in
  the First World War, 1914–1918.
  1. World War, 1914–1918——Women——Great
  Britain   2. Women——Great Britain——Social
  conditions
  I. Condell, Diana   II. Liddiard, Jean
  305.4'2'0941   DA639.W7
ISBN 0–7102–0974–6

CONTENTS

Acknowledgements   xiii
Authors' note   xv
Introduction: Britain before 1914   1

1 The domestic sphere expands   7
2 Beyond the traditional feminine role   21
3 From response to initiative   55
4 From family to factory   73
5 Servants of the state   115
6 From housewife to heroine   157

Abbreviations   187
Chronology   189
Appendix 1   Note on the official photographers   193
Appendix 2   Libraries and archives holding manuscript
                 collections and photographs   194
Select bibliography   195
Index   197

ILLUSTRATIONS

1	A scene on the Course, Derby Day	6
2	Girl worker fastening dolls' wigs in a toy factory, 1918	9
3	Mrs Rosanna Forster carrying on her husband's business as a chimney-sweep in Kent	10
4	Girl carrying on her father's appointment of official bill poster and town crier, Thetford	10
5	Woman funeral hearse driver	11
6	A woman carrying on her husband's duties as a gravedigger	11
7	Princess Beatrice, Queen Mary and Princess Mary receiving gifts for sailors and soldiers, 1917	12
8	Dr R. Murray Leslie lecturing to Red Cross nurses, 1914	13
9	Mrs Mapstone-Graham, Corps Commandant at the Scottish Women's First Aid Corps Camp, Gosford, 1914	14
10	Inside Hilders Hospital, Haslemere, c. 1917	15
11	Schoolgirls with vegetables grown on their own allotments	16
12	Girl Guides signalling	17
13	King George V and Queen Mary digging potatoes, 1917	18
14	A ward in Constance, Duchess of Westminster's Hospital, Le Touquet, 1917	19
15	A nursing member of the Voluntary Aid Detachment	20
16	Interior of a ward on a British Ambulance Train, near Doullens, 1918	23
17	Interior view of the Princess Victoria Rest Club for Nurses, Etaples, 1917	24
18	Competitors arriving for a fishing contest, Watten, 1918	26
19	Fishing contest between nurses of hospital barges, Watten, 1918	27
20	Four nursing sisters and a Royal Army Medical Corps Captain, 1918	27
21	Dr Patterson and Miss North at 25 Stationary Hospital, Rouen	28
22	The Prince of Wales at the Duchess of Sutherland's Hospital at Calais, 1917	29
23	Gas cases on a hospital train near Béthune, 1918	30
24	German ward of 4 Stationary Hospital, Longuenesse	31
25	A German prisoner having his wounded hand dressed in the VAD dressing station at Abbéville, 1917	31
26	Dame Maud McCarthy, Matron-in-Chief of Queen Alexandra's Imperial Military Nursing Service, 1918	32
27	TFNS nursing sister talking to a wounded soldier at Dernacourt, 1916	33
28	Patients playing cards outside the Australian Hospital, Mudros	34

29 Army nurses and VADs aboard the hospital ship *St Andrew*   36
30 Damage done during the air raids on the Hospital Area, Etaples,
   1918   36
31 Funeral of a nursing sister killed during the bombing of Etaples,
   1918   37
32 Edith Cavell with her dogs   39
33 The Baroness de T'Serclaes and Miss Mairi Chisholm,
   Ramscapelle, 1917   40
34 Sergeant-Major Flora Sandes, Salonika, 1917   41
35 Dr Elsie Maud Inglis   42
36 Dr G. Eleanor Soltau, Chief Medical Officer at Kragujevac   43
37 Dr Beatrice McGregor and Miss Pares, Serbia   43
38 No. 32 Stationary Hospital at Wimereux   44
39 Members of the First Aid Nursing Yeomanry serving as
   ambulance drivers, Calais, 1918   46
40 Mabel Ann Stobart Greenhalgh   47
41 FANY ambulance drivers in their fur coats, Calais, 1917   48
42 VAD drivers, Boulogne, attending to the maintenance of their
   cars, 1918   50
43 Member of the Women's Hospital Corps, Endell Street, 1918   50
44 Mrs McDougal, Organising Officer of the FANY   51
45 Dr Dorothy Hare, Assistant Medical Director, Women's Royal
   Naval Service, 1918   52
46 The Women's Royal Air Force in France, Maresquel, 1919   53
47 Member of Glasgow Battalion of the Women's Volunteer Reserve,
   1915   54
48 Uniform worn by officer and private, Women's Volunteer Reserve   57
49 Lady Major Egger of the Lady Instructors' Signals Company,
   1918   57
50 Lannock Summer Camp, 1916   58
51 Women's Legion: a member of the Agricultural Section, 1918   60
52 Women's Auxiliary Force: Highbury Branch members working
   on their allotments, *c.* 1915   61
53 Procession of women demanding the right to enter the war
   services, 1915   62
54 Women's Legion: a member of the Canteen Section, 1918   63
55 Women's Police Patrol outside Euston Station   64
56 Women's Police Patrols, *c.* 1916   65
57 Mrs Theo Stanley, Superior of Special Women's Patrols   66
58 Margaret Damer Dawson, OBE, Commandant of the Women's
   Police Service, with the Sub-Commandant Mary S. Allen, OBE,
   c. 1917   67
59 Nurses tending a slight casualty in a shell filling factory, *c.* 1917   68
60 Queen Mary visiting Woolwich Babies' Home, 1917   69
61 Henriette Maud Fraser of the FANY, with Mrs Hamilton
   Lawrence   70
62 Margaret Bondfield   71
63 Estelle Sylvia Pankhurst   71
64 Women coal workers in a Lancashire colliery, 1918   72
65 Woman worker cutting shives in the cooperage of a London
   brewery, 1918   74
66 Woman worker using a blow-torch to solder cigarette tins,
   Birmingham, 1918   75

67 Women in the hand finishing shop at the linoleum works,
   Kirkcaldy, Fife, 1918   76
68 Women workers sorting shirts and underclothing at the
   Dewsbury branch of the Army Ordnance Department, 1917   76
69 Textile worker winding cotton in a Nottingham lace factory,
   1918   77
70 Women chopping and bundling kindling wood, *c.* 1918   77
71 Women packing flour, Birkenhead, Lancashire, 1918   80
72 Workers at the caustic soda works, Warrington, Lancashire,
   1918   80
73 Women workers for Glasgow Gas Department emptying a coal
   wagon, 1918   81
74 Labourers employed by Glasgow Gas Department cleaning
   firebricks, 1918   81
75 Young workers preparing filter cloths for the sugar presses,
   Greenock, 1918   84
76 Woman worker spreading refined sugar before bagging, Glebe
   Sugar Refinery, Greenock, Scotland, 1918   84
77 Workers stacking barrels at the oil and seed cake works,
   Silvertown, London, 1918   85
78 Women employees cleaning retort mouthpieces, Glasgow Gas
   Department, 1918   85
79 Women porters, Goods Department, South East & Chatham
   Railway Company Depot, London, 1918   88
80 Leather workers at the Pavlova Leather Company's tanning
   works, Abingdon, Berkshire, 1918   89
81 London General Omnibus Company conductress in summer
   uniform, 1918   90
82 Women ticket collectors at the Great Western Railway Terminus,
   Paddington, 1915   91
83 Postwomen outside a district sorting office   92
84 Woman parcel truck driver, Great Eastern Railway Company,
   1918   93
85 Woman guard on a London Underground train, 1918   93
86 Window cleaners for the Mayfair Window Cleaning Company,
   1918   94
87 A shipyard worker and her horse at the Govan Shipyard on the
   Clyde, 1918   95
88 Trades delivery girls in South London, 1915   96
89 Women workers at Messrs Thew, Hooker Silby Ltd,
   Buckinghamshire, 1918   97
90 Employees of the South East Chatham Railway leaving their
   depot, Old Kent Road, London, 1918   97
91 Corporation of Glasgow Tramways Department, Electrical Sub-
   Station Attendant, 1918   98
92 Assistant in charge of the Receiving Room, Glasgow Corporation
   Weights and Measures Department, 1918   99
93 A woman fitter at work in the London General Omnibus
   Company's workshops, 1918   100
94 Worker operating a machine for centering studded tread on
   motor tyres, Manchester, 1918   101
95 Women retort house workers, South Metropolitan Gas Co.,
   London, 1918   102

 96 Women carpenters employed by Tarrants to construct huts for
    British troops, 1918   102
 97 Shipyard workers, Palmers Shipbuilding Yard, Hebburn-on-
    Tyne, *c.* 1918   103
 98 Women workers sewing asbestos mattresses used for lining
    boilers in battleships, Messrs Turner Brothers Asbestos Factory,
    Trafford Park, Manchester, 1918   103
 99 Men and women workers filling shells at the Chilwell Factory,
    Nottingham, 1918   106
100 Miss Lilian Barker, OBE, with women workers in the TNT
    Department, Woolwich Arsenal, 1918   106
101 A woman worker acetylene welding the body of an aerial bomb,
    1918   107
102 Woman worker fitting sections to the templates of aeroplane
    propellers, Frederick Tibbenham Ltd, Suffolk, *c.* 1918   108
103 Women workers at Vickers Ltd, 1917   110
104 Operator hand stemming a 9.2 inch high explosive artillery shell
    after filling with Amatol, Hereford, 1917   111
105 Munitions workers filling machine gun ammunition belts at the
    Park Royal Factory, north-west London, *c.* 1918   112
106 Funeral procession of a munitions worker killed on duty,
    Swansea, 1917   113
107 Members of the Women's Army Auxiliary Corps employed in the
    Army bakery, Dieppe, 1918   114
108 Ratings of the Women's Royal Naval Service serving in the
    canteen at the Royal Marine Barracks, Chatham, Kent, 1918   117
109 WRNS Ratings, based at Lowestoft on the Suffolk coast, painting
    mines and steel floats, 1918   118
110 Members of the Women's Army Auxiliary Corps in their mess
    room, Rouen, 1917   119
111 Women's Army Auxiliary Corps Cooks tending fat boilers in an
    infantry camp, Rouen, 1917   120
112 WAACs tending presses in the Army Printing Works, Abbéville,
    France, 1917   121
113 Women's Royal Naval Service Ratings in their quarters at Osea
    Island, Essex, 1918   122
114 Locator Card Section, Queen Mary's Army Auxiliary Corps with
    the American Expeditionary Force at Bourges. On the left is Miss
    Bigge, and on the right, Miss Starr   124
115 WRNS Officer instructing Ratings in the use of Anti-Gas
    Respirators, Lowestoft, 1918   125
116 Members of the Queen Mary's Army Auxiliary Corps working in
    the stores office at the 61st Advanced Motor Transport Section at
    Abbéville, 1919   126
117 Queen Mary's Army Auxiliary Corps Camp No. 4, Rouen, a
    general view of the Nissen Huts, 1919   127
118 WRNS Ratings storewomen sorting ships' lamps at Lowestoft,
    1918   129
119 Ratings of the Women's Royal Naval Service, *HMS Victory*,
    Crystal Palace, Sydenham, 1918   130
120 Dame Katherine Furse, GBE, Director WRNS, and her Secretary,
    Miss M. Butcher, MBE, 1918   130
121 Recreation room at WRNS Quarters, Osea Island, 1918   132

122 WRNS Record Office, Stanhope Gate, London, 1918   132
123 Members of the Women's Royal Air Force boarding Air Force
     tenders to go to their billets in Cologne, 1919   134
124 WAAC Drivers attending to the engine of an officer's car,
     Abbéville, 1917   137
125 Women Air Mechanics of the Women's Royal Air Force working
     on the fuselage of the AVRO 540, probably 1919   138
126 Woman Motor Driver serving with the Royal Flying Corps, *c.*
     1917   140
127 Women's Royal Air Force Clerk, 1919   141
128 Members of the Women's Forestry Corps stripping the bark off
     trees, Cross in Hand, Heathfield, Sussex, 1918   142
129 Two members of the Women's Forestry Corps grinding an axe,
     Cross in Hand, Heathfield, Sussex, 1918   143
130 Women horse trainers, at Rimington's Establishment at
     Shrewsbury, 1919   144
131 A woman horse trainer at Rimington's, administering what
     Nicholls called 'the earclutch method to prevent escaping
     proclivities', 1919   145
132 Woman farm worker feeding poultry, possibly near Langstock,
     in Hampshire, 1918   146
133 Members of the Women's Forage Corps feeding a hay baler,
     Middlesex, 1918   148
134 Members of the Women's Land Army starting out for work, Dens
     Farm, Harefield, nr Uxbridge, Middlesex, probably 1918   149
135 WLA member watering her horses, Dens Farm, 1918   150
136 Women's Land Army member with a team of horses ploughing,
     Dens Farm, Harefield, nr Uxbridge, Middlesex, 1918   151
137 Women's Forestry Corps member in uniform, 1918   152
138 Women forestry workers, Cross in Hand, Heathfield, Sussex, with
     logs loaded on to a sledge for transportation to the stacks, 1918   153
139 Princess Mary picking fruit in Frogmore Gardens, watched by
     Queen Mary, 1917   154
140 Typical girl flax puller, Barwick, 1918   155
141 Woman window cleaner employed by the Mayfair Window
     Cleaning Co. Ltd, 1918   156
142 Woman railway carriage cleaner using a vacuum cleaner,
     London terminus, 1918   158
143 Woman gas lamp cleaner on the railways, 1918   159
144 Women labourers employed by the Lancashire and Yorkshire
     Railway, Manchester, cleaning the glass on the roof of Clifton
     Power Station, 1917   161
145 Women glass workers in Lancashire in the sludge pits treating
     the residue from the sand-working tables, 1918   161
146 Girls packing electric light bulbs at a factory in Birmingham, *c.*
     1918   162
147 Woman attendant employed in a bacteriological laboratory
     located in the works of Messrs Lyle & Co., 1918   163
148 Woman railway worker operating signals in a cabin on a siding,
     Great Central Railway, Birmingham, 1918   164
149 A woman motor lorry driver employed by Glasgow Tramways
     Department, 1917   165
150 Women workers tar-spraying a London street, probably 1918   166

151 Members of the women's Fire Brigade at a Middlesex munitions
     factory, 1918   166
152 Woman granite worker employed on sand-blasting at Messrs
     Stewart & Co. Ltd, Fraser Place, Aberdeen, Scotland, 1918   167
153 Mrs Gerard Barnes, WRNS motor-boat driver, with her dog,
     Southwick, Sussex, 1918   170
154 Woman railway porter on the London South Eastern & Chatham
     Railway dealing with two calves, *c.* 1917   171
155 A Forestry Corps Forewoman with her two children, Cross in
     Hand, Heathfield, Sussex, 1918   173
156 Olive Edis Galsworthy, known as Olive Edis, 1876–1955   174
157 'Palmer Munitionettes', the women's football team made up of
     employees of the Palmers Shipbuilding Co. Ltd, Hebburn-on-
     Tyne, 1918   175
158 Off-duty members of the WAAC going down to bathe at Paris
     Plage, 1917   177
159 VAD Christmas entertainment, at Constance, Duchess of
     Westminster's Hospital, France, 1917   177
160 WAACs and soldiers on the edge of a crater caused by an enemy
     bomb dropped in their camp during an air raid at Abbéville,
     1918   178
161 WAACs tending the graves of British soldiers in a cemetery,
     Abbéville, 1918   181
162 Women munition workers in Swansea mourning the death of a
     colleague killed in an accident at work, 1917   183
163 WAAC gardeners tending the graves of war dead, Etaples, 1919   184

ACKNOWLEDGEMENTS

The authors gratefully acknowledge the gracious permission of Her Majesty The Queen to consult material in the Royal Archive and to reproduce photographs from Queen Mary's private album.

They also wish to acknowledge the following: Trustees of the Imperial War Museum; Trustees of the National Portrait Gallery and the Royal Photographic Society, for permission to reproduce photographs from their collections.

Finally they wish to thank the following individuals for help and support: Giles Gordon, Rachel Morris, Andrew Wheatcroft, Jane Carmichael, Michael Collinson, Dorothy Scott-Stevenson.

AUTHORS' NOTE

The Imperial War Museum was founded in 1917 as the result of a War Cabinet decision to record the nation's effort in the First World War. (Originally known as the National War Museum, its name was changed at the request of representatives from the Empire.) From the outset women's war work was recognised as an integral part of it. The Women's Work Sub-Committee set about collecting all kinds of material for the national collection, including photographs. Some of these were specially commissioned from established photographers such as Horace W. Nicholls, G. P. Lewis and Olive Edis, the only woman photographer represented. These, together with photographs acquired from other sources, form a unique and wide-ranging visual record of the work of women on all fronts in the First World War. Although there is material on the subject elsewhere, notably the Fawcett Library and the Public Record Office, the Imperial War Museum collection is so rich and diverse as well as relatively unknown that we felt it appropriate to concentrate on that source. There are some 4,000 photographs on this topic, most of them of superb quality, and for each one chosen here a dozen were rejected.

The aim of the book is to tell the story of the First World War as it appeared to women, and to illustrate the many and varied roles played by them in the war effort which have been largely forgotten in the intervening years. It is significant because this experience did change women's perception of themselves and their own place in society, as well as that society's view of them. Because cultural responses to women, now as then, are especially attuned to their physical appearance (which is itself of course subject to fashion and historical change), developments in the visual image of women have particular implications for assessing their place in the social structure of their time. The photographs in this book have been arranged thematically rather than chronologically in order to let this emerge with strength and clarity from the visual evidence.

INTRODUCTION

Britain before 1914

The First World War marked the great division in British consciousness between the modern, familiar twentieth century and the pre-war world with its roots deep in Edwardian and Victorian Britain. As the war initiated society into the unprecedented horrors of modern technological warfare, the popular reaction has naturally been to endow that now-distant world with a golden mythic quality born of nostalgia. Yet the horrors of war had their counterpart in peace. The industrial revolution which had led to modern war had also created the sprawling industrial cities that sucked the population from the countryside into the factories, plunging them into the slum conditions that became a symbol of appalling exploitation and poverty. The poet William Blake was one of the first to express this sense of darkness and unease underlying the dynamic wealth which the new industry also created, in juxtaposing 'England's green and pleasant land' with 'those dark satanic mills'. The power of both those concepts has dominated the British imagination for two centuries and the photographers represented here were also shaped by them.

By the time of Queen Victoria's death in 1901, Great Britain was ostensibly the richest and most powerful nation on earth. By 1911 the population had risen to over 40 million and the nation, with the exception of Ireland, had become a heavily industrialised and mainly urban society, centred on the coal-producing areas in the north of England, South Wales, the Scottish lowlands and the Midlands. Although the major industries – iron, steel, textiles and coal – were still generating enormous wealth, competition from the United States and Germany was already threatening the overseas markets. The middle classes who owed their very existence to the growth of industry began to move out of the smoky centres of the large cities to the pleasant leafy suburbs. Houses became more comfortable, gardens became larger, and, with servants to do the housework and cooking, the middle classes enjoyed a social round which quietly mirrored that enjoyed on a grander scale by the upper classes in their London houses and on their country estates. By 1911 agriculture was in decline and farming as a livelihood occupied less than 21 per cent of the population. The British Empire was the source of cheap food imports which made home production of staple commodities uneconomic. The countryside, from which many had emerged two generations before, now became the goal to which they aspired. Creating the comforts of middle-class life in rural surroundings was made possible now by a well-developed system of roads and railways.

The greatest centre of population, however, and the focus of the nation's political and cultural life was the capital, London. Some 8 million people lived within the greater London area, and as the capital also of the British Empire it enjoyed enormous wealth and prestige. Business and finance were centred in the City of London, but political power lay along the Thames at Westminster. Although the 1911 Reform Act had curbed some of the powers of the House of Lords, its members nevertheless remained the pivot on which the élite and aspiring classes of British society turned. That Britain was a strongly class-structured society is patently clear from contemporary sources; that it was class-conscious in the modern sense is less clear. There was a well-established working-class radical tradition closely linked with the development of the trade unions and the evangelicalism of Non-Conformist religion which had led to the establishment of the fledgling Labour Party; from this sprang the first militant women's suffrage group, the Women's Social and Political Union, led by the Pankhurst family who had worked for the Labour movement in Manchester. Yet although it was the British working-class experience which was studied by political theorists and activists who saw revolution as the inevitable solution to the vast inequalities of wealth and class, the majority of British people did not seem to want radical social upheaval. They sought to improve their lot within the existing structure, fighting for better pay and improved conditions, rather than dismantling it and losing their sense of identity and security. The broad contemporary view defined the working classes as all wage earners getting less than the Income Tax threshold of £160 per annum. They formed 80 per cent of society; the middle classes were seen as a flexible group of anything between 10 and 18 per cent, and the remainder was upper class. Certainly by 1913 the line between the better-off members of the working class and the lower end of the middle class was becoming increasingly blurred. Yet the working classes, so vast and so potentially powerful, were becoming more and more dissatisfied with their share of the nation's wealth, most of which was concentrated in the upper 20 per cent of the population. The antiquated franchise system disqualified most of them – more than four-fifths – from the vote and therefore from political power.

There was another section of society which was wholly dis-enfranchised, yet which cut across all class divisions: women. The achieving of the vote came to symbolise for them not only political power but a growing sense of their exclusion from opportunity in a rapidly changing world. This was exacerbated by traditional male perceptions as to what it was right and proper for a woman to be or to do. Active and extreme discontent was not widespread, but in every sphere of life the pace was quickening, and many well-educated women, increasing in number, now felt that they could contribute far more to society than had hitherto been deemed appropriate. To the frequent cry that women wanted the vote without the responsibilities of emancipation, the women's movement responded that its main energy came from the wish to give rather than take. Those women freed from want by higher economic and social status were motivated by a desire to better the lot of their less-privileged sisters rather than to seize direct political power for their own benefit. They had been brought up in the Victorian philanthropic tradition and it was often the confrontation with the domestic and working conditions of working women and their families that caused them to start thinking in political terms: 'We want the vote to stop the white slave traffic, sweated labour and to save the children' (slogan from a WSPU poster).

Many upper-class women did exercise very considerable political influence, but in most cases it was through their status as the wives of prominent men. The great political hostesses of the period wielded considerable power, but it sprang from their social position, not their rights as citizens. The state certainly needed the economic contribution of women, for example in the textile industry, but it did not need their approval for its actions, nor did it demand from them any obligation in a wider abstract sense. It was here that the war wrought one of the most fundamental changes in the position of women, although the seeds of that change had been sown before the war started.

The deep divisions in British society (which was also under potential threat from the beginnings of unrest within the Empire) were manifesting themselves in agitation and discontent: where the women's movement was concerned the non-violent work of the National Union of Women's Suffrage Societies was eclipsed by the sensational tactics of the new militant Women's Social and Political Union – the suffragettes. Yet it was still in general terms a stable society with a respect for the law and a sense of place for the individual. The state gave no direct support or aid to the underprivileged with which the country swarmed, but nor did it make many demands on them either.

The idea of nation and Empire was a general if dimly understood source of pride for the multitude to whom it offered little that was tangible. No man was required to serve the state and bear arms in its defence unless he chose, and the 8 million or so enfranchised citizens were not obliged to cast their votes. The multiplicity of rules, regulations and by-laws characteristic of late-twentieth-century society was quite absent before 1914. The state impinged on all individuals only at their birth and death and, through the church, at their marriage. For virtually all women this, together with the births of their children, was likely to be their only direct contact with the state. (The ceremony and expense of formal marriage were frequently dispensed with in many working-class households, as will be seen later.) Women of all classes shared a dependent status before the law, with the exception of wealthy women for whom independent financial provision was made even when they married.

The business of nation and Empire was the province of men; apart from endemic political trouble in Ireland and the small if newsworthy band of suffragettes, most women and their families were concerned as usual with private affairs. Wars happened overseas, in Europe or far-flung outposts of Empire, and when the news broke of the assassination of the heir to the Austro-Hungarian Empire in Sarajevo, Serbia, most people were not interested. The majority had never heard of Serbia and knew nothing of the political and military issues involved, let alone of the upheaval that was to take place in their own lives. It was high summer, the weather was unusually warm, and the August Bank Holiday beckoned.

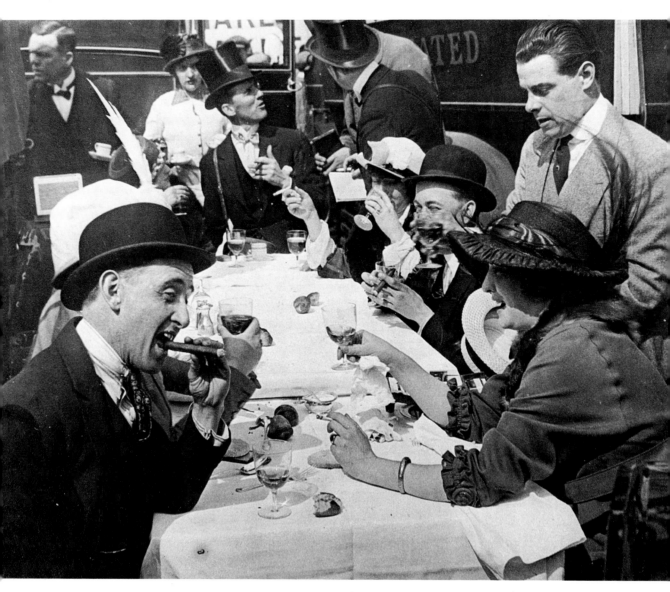

PLATE 1
A scene on the Course, Derby Day

One of a famous series of pre-war Derby Day photographs by the professional photographer Horace W. Nicholls, this study captures the sunny expansive quality now popularly associated with the period. The great annual race meeting on Epsom Downs, and Derby Day in particular, was one of the few public occasions attended by all social classes, when the very rich and the very poor shared the same outdoor summer pleasures. Here the diners and waiters would probably all at the time have been considered working class (according to one contemporary definition, as being below the Income Tax threshold of £160 per annum). The women's hats and the men's bowlers were formal Sunday-best dress; the top hats and cravats imitated upper-class attire, but no true 'toff' would have graced this modest gathering. Upper- and middle-class women would not have smoked in public at this period.

Photographer: Horace W. Nicholls
Source: RPS no. 7674

CHAPTER I

THE DOMESTIC SPHERE EXPANDS

'Womanhood Offers Her Gifts At Her Country's Door'
(Caption on a woman's suffrage banner)

'Let us prove ourselves worthy of citizenship, whether our claim be recognised or not,' wrote Millicent Garrett Fawcett, President of the National Union of Women's Suffrage Societies to her members on the NUWSS decision to suspend political suffrage agitation to concentrate on the war effort. Her words signalled the profound change the war was to initiate for women. Although many of the transformations were to prove temporary, the movement of women from the private to the public world and the acknowledgement of a new relationship with the state would become permanent. Women might return to the domestic sphere, but the door to the outside remained open.

The first steps taken by women were in response to circumstances over which, as so often, they had no control. The outbreak of war in August 1914 brought two immediate consequences for all women without financial independence, who were of course the great majority. As the Services started recruiting in earnest, many women lost their men to the military, with a consequent drop in income. There was a pensions and allowance system operated by the War Office which was so antiquated that it was based on figures unchanged since the Boer War fifteen years before. Secondly, to add to the loss of the breadwinner, the initial economic disruption caused widespread unemployment, particularly among women who were then as now the most vulnerable section of the work force, unprotected by the male trade unions or by any welfare system. Those employed in the infamous 'sweated trades', notably dressmaking and millinery, were the first casualties of the war; ironically it was the patriotic determination of wealthy women to abstain from fripperies that threw their labouring sisters out of work.

The largest concentration of reasonably well-paid women in industry was in the textile trades, which would also be affected by the war; the second-largest area of female employment was domestic service, where women, although initially untouched by immediate job losses, would eventually leave as large households were scaled down under wartime conditions and as other job opportunities beckoned from 1915 onwards. To the general public the first visible sign of change in the lot of working women was not their unemployment, by its nature an invisible condition, but the fact that women simply took the place of their absent men and carried on with their jobs. Some wives and daughters continued the small businesses like chimney-sweeping or blacksmith's work with which they would have assisted their men in peacetime anyway; others persuaded employers to let them undertake the job vacated by husband or father which would both continue to bring in a wage (though probably not equal to the man's) and, even more important, would keep the job open for the man on his return from the war.

The women of the middle and upper classes were not immune from the same patriotic enthusiasm firing their men. Although they did not on the whole have the financial worries of their working-class sisters, they shared for the first time a similar situation of losing their men to the war in increasing numbers and finding that the country had made little or no provision for women or for utilising their efforts. Thus, while the state organised the men of all classes, the women organised themselves. Initially middle- and upper-class women naturally turned to the skills they had acquired in peacetime, just as the chimney-sweep's wife did, but in their case it was raising money and running charitable ventures. Apart from such fashionable and immediate causes as the Belgian and Serbian Relief Funds and the succour of Belgian refugees, much of their effort went to aiding women. Here the pre-war suffrage organisations came into their own. The NUWSS, for example, took up the cause of inadequate pensions and separation allowances for the dependants of servicemen – including the problem that surfaced early in the war of women living with servicemen but not in fact married to them. The NUWSS won the battle of their entitlement to the appropriate allowances – an early sign that the official image of Victorian womanhood was beginning to crack under the stress of war. The NUWSS Women's Interest's Committee and the Women's Emergency Corps (founded by radical suffragettes and respectable aristocratic ladies), whether they opposed or supported the cause of war, were united in the belief that the rights of women and their families should not be eroded but improved through the war effort. Such organisations had set aside the suffrage struggle in the national emergency and turned their considerable expertise into practical ways of alleviating the crisis for women. For example, according to a report on 15 May 1915 in the *Lady's Pictorial* the NUWSS was engaged in the following: directing women into vacant jobs; examining police regulations on the sale of intoxicating liquor to women; pressing the Government to set up a register of women for war work; and recruiting women police.

The moderate and the radical both found that the war was altering the social landscape, bringing together women with common concerns across the social divide. The most dramatic example of this was the unexpected liaison forged between Queen Mary and the radical founder and Secretary of the Women's Trades Union League, Mary Macarthur (it was nicknamed 'the strange case of Mary M and Mary R'). The Queen had soon grasped that the war had brought major unemployment to women in the sweated trades, and asked to meet Mary Macarthur to co-operate in setting up the Central Committee for Women's Training and Employment; their mutual respect and understanding was immediate. On 20 August 1914 they launched The Queen's Work For Women Fund 'in the firm belief that the prevention of distress is better than its relief, and employment is better than charity'. Following the royal lead, most middle- and upper-class women not only organised comforts for the troops but raised enormous sums of money for the welfare of servicemen and their families and the relief of economic distress. The notion of Ladies Bountiful dispensing charity was traditional, and had already come to be resented by many, including women involved in pre-war political activities. Yet Britain at that period had little social welfare and of course no National Health Service and was quite unprepared for the demands of modern warfare particularly on its limited medical facilities, and it was largely the efforts of women which funded the medical charities like the British Red Cross, which became indispensable in providing hospitals and staff.

PLATE 2

Girl worker fastening dolls' wigs in a toy factory, 1918

Child labour was still widespread in Britain before and during the First World War. Legal enforcement of school attendance was variable and employers, for cheapness, encouraged 'half timers': children who worked in factories for up to 33 hours a week and went to school the rest of the time. Toymaking was akin to the notorious 'sweated trades' largely involving women and children who toiled long hours for a pittance from piecework; the pre-war women's movement had campaigned against their exploitation. Here in 1918 this young girl is working in comfortless squalid conditions as bad as any before the war. G. P. Lewis has caught the implicit pathos of the girl young enough to play with dolls trapped in the drudgery of their manufacture. Yet toymaking was the first solution to female unemployment found by the Women's Emergency Corps in the autumn of 1914, though they aimed at better conditions and a reasonable rate of pay.

Photographer: G. P. Lewis
Source: IWM Q28158

PLATE 3 *Above left*

Mrs Rosanna Forster carrying on her husband's business as a chimney-sweep in Kent

This and the following three photographs are from Nicholls's war work on 'substitution': women taking over men's jobs to release the latter for military service. The wives of the self-employed like Mrs Forster had always helped their husbands run their businesses, but had rarely taken (or been acknowledged as taking) sole control.

Photographer: Horace W. Nicholls
Source: IWM Q30761

PLATE 4 *Above right*

Girl carrying on her father's appointment of official bill poster and town crier, Thetford, Norfolk

The traditional view of women as defined by their relationship to their men – wife, mother, daughter, sister – was still prevalent during the war as the contemporary captions show. For the majority of women and their families their livelihood was so precarious and so bound up with their menfolk's that the chance to undertake the latter's jobs was eagerly seized. This was not only to ensure an income in the man's absence but to secure the future. Many employers agreed to keep a man's job for him on his return from the war if a woman would do it in the meantime; both understood that the situation was temporary. The posters in the photograph emphasise this: one calls for women to join the Queen Mary's Army Auxiliary Corps, others for men over military age to volunteer for Home Defence and so 'help the boys abroad'.

Photographer: Horace W. Nicholls
Source: IWM Q31028

PLATE 5 *Above left*
Woman funeral hearse driver

The impact of Nicholls's image comes from the dramatic tension between the ceremonial funeral trappings and the shock of recognising a woman in the masculine garb of top hat, driving coat and high boots. She is also professionally rather than privately participating in the public show of mourning where traditionally the women were veiled from view in black to mark a private expression of grief.

Photographer: Horace W. Nicholls
Source: IWM Q31127

PLATE 6 *Above right*
A woman carrying on her husband's duties as a gravedigger during his absence abroad

Although Nicholls, who had an official government commission, naturally tended to present women as cheerful and determined in their occupations so unfamiliar to the public notion of womanhood (if not to the women themselves), he also revealed the arduousness of the work. The exhaustion lining the gravedigger's face is as much a counter to the ideal of the delicate incapable female as the grimly basic nature of the work.

Photographer: Horace W. Nicholls
Source: IWM Q31237

PLATE 7

Left to right: **Princess Beatrice, Queen Mary and Princess Mary receiving gifts for sailors and soldiers on behalf of Queen Mary's Needlework Guild at Friary Court, St James's Palace, 8 June 1917**

Queen Mary's Needlework Guild had before the war organised needlework for charitable purposes. From 1914 it collected and distributed clothing, surgical supplies, books and other articles for the relief of servicemen and their families. The Royal ladies found that their pre-war charity work now assumed great importance: privately raised funds became essential for the relief of economic distress exacerbated especially for women by the outbreak of war, and to fill the gaps in government provision for the welfare of the troops, such as the basic equipping and staffing of hospitals. Queen Alexandra's 'Alexandra Rose Day', instituted before the war, was the first charity appeal to sell tokens on the streets. Its success ensured its survival to the present day and set the pattern for fund-raising, to which most upper-class women now devoted their pre-war charitable skills.

Photographer: Unknown
Source: Royal Archives, Queen Mary's Photograph Albums

PLATE 8
Dr R. Murray Leslie lecturing to Red Cross nurses in training at the Institute of Hygiene, September 1914

Middle- and upper-class women desired as much as their menfolk to share in the patriotic excitement of wartime activity, but apart from utilising their traditional 'good works' to wartime ends there were no immediate outlets for them. Care of the sick, however, was recognised as central to the role of women, and many joined the international charities of the British Red Cross Society and the Order of St John of Jerusalem. The work was voluntary and unpaid, which clearly excluded women who had to support themselves or others; the women here are in better health and better dressed than their working-class sisters.

Photographer: Unknown
Source: IWM Q53310

PLATE 9

Mrs Mapstone-Graham *right*, **Corps Commandant at the Scottish Women's First Aid Corps Camp, Gosford,** *c.* **1914**

For the first time in history well-to-do women now wanted actively to participate in the war effort: the notion of 'service' to King and country moved them as it did their men. Unable like the latter to join official bodies, they simply organised their own quasi-military groups, with a hierarchy of 'officers' and 'other ranks'. The aim at first was to act in a supportive, but still subordinate, role to their men. At this early stage, however, living 'under canvas' did not mean forgoing the accepted comforts of middle- and upper-class homes, as the presence of good china and cutlery laid out for 'kit' inspection confirms.

Photographer: Unknown
Source: IWM Q108103

PLATE 10
Inside Hilders Hospital, Haslemere, *c.* 1917. *Left*: the Almeric Paget masseuse, Miss Scoones, with a patient; *right*: Sister Emerson who became Matron in 1918

One of the new early civilian organisations to be accepted by the War Office was the Military Massage Corps founded by Mr and Mrs Almeric Paget who supplied – and paid – fifty trained masseuses for work with the war wounded. By 1915 they had gained official recognition and from 1917 they were working in France. There were 2,000 by November 1918. The work shown here is clearly related to the modern treatment of physiotherapy. Miss Scoones is wearing the Corps badge on her sleeve. Hilders was a house belonging to Lord and Lady Aberconway.

Photographer: Unknown
Source: IWM Q108081

PLATE 11 *Above*
Schoolgirls with vegetables grown on their own allotments

The economic disruption at the outbreak of war resulted in rising prices, especially of such imported foods as meat and sugar. For the average unskilled worker's family the cost of living rose by 81 per cent between 1914 and 1918, and for the average skilled man's family by 67 per cent. This and eventual shortages reinforced the perennial problem of the unbalanced working-class diet. So the population, like these schoolgirls, were encouraged to produce their own fresh vegetables, though the working classes, lacking gardens, obviously had little opportunity to do so.

Photographer: Horace W. Nicholls
Source: IWM Q31154

PLATE 12 *Right*
Girl Guides signalling

As the Victorian girls' public schools modelled themselves on those of their brothers, so in the Edwardian period the Girl Guide movement was founded in imitation of the Boy Scouts. Although to some feminists this meant that young girls were being inducted into the hearty regimentation they so deplored in male organisations, others recognised that the practical uniforms and chance of outdoor pursuits away from parents and governesses and nannies offered middle-class girls some freedom at least from the old feminine constraints, as this image surely shows. The Girl Guides were the one female uniformed organisation at the outbreak of war familiar with the semi-military activities of their brothers.

Photographer: Horace W. Nicholls
Source: IWM Q30965

PLATE 13
King George V and Queen Mary digging potatoes, Windsor, spring 1917

By 1917 food shortages and consequent queues for basic foodstuffs were growing, and were greater in some areas than in others. No systematic rationing system was introduced in the First World War, but in the autumn of 1917 the Government subsidised and stabilised the price of bread, still the staple food of the working classes. In 1918 they introduced meat rationing and a new word, 'coupon', a token cut from the rationing card. Potatoes were also subsidised in 1917, and the King and Queen with typical conscientiousness took part in a nationally encouraged effort to produce more. This unusual informal family snap from Queen Mary's album must surely provide the only glimpse of a king in braces. The sense of intimacy rare in royal images of this period gives it a particular charm.

Photographer: Unknown
Source: Royal Archives, Queen Mary's Photograph Albums

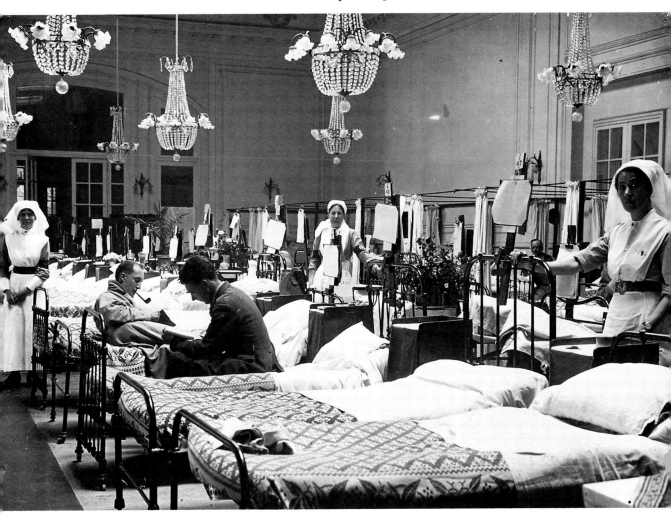

PLATE 14
A ward in Constance, Duchess of Westminster's (no. 1 Red Cross) Hospital, Le Touquet, 18 June 1917

The Duchess of Westminster, like the Duchess of Sutherland, was one of many aristocratic women who responded to the war by extending their peacetime roles of leading charitable organisers. Their pre-eminent social position and wealth gave them a network of influential contacts which they determinedly used to implement their plans. Thus the Duchess of Sutherland set up her first hospital abroad in Dunkirk as early as October 1914. Here at Le Touquet the chandeliers and decorative mouldings of the ward show that the hospital was housed in an hotel or château. In Britain also patriotic ladies put large – and often inconvenient – country houses at the disposal of the medical authorities.

Photographer: Unknown
Source: IWM Q2405

PLATE 15
A nursing member of the Voluntary Aid Detachment

Nicholls entitled this portrait 'Reverie: a Red Cross Worker' and the romantic title and prettily posed figure of the young VAD clearly reveal how the role of women as nurses was perceived as reassuringly 'feminine'. The starched cotton uniform relates to the nun's habit, the traditional attire of the dedicated woman. The faintly virginal religious aura is strengthened by the Madonna lilies in the background – the photographer here has borrowed from painting a traditional symbolic attribute revitalised by the Pre-Raphaelites. The Voluntary Aid Detachments (hence VADs) were enlisted from 1910 by the two medical charities of the Red Cross and the Order of St John to supplement inadequate professional nursing services. By 1916 some 8,000 VADs were employed in various tasks, but it was the nurses who caught the popular imagination. Their acceptability prepared the public for more radical departures later on.

Photographer: Horace W. Nicholls
Source: IWM Q31011

CHAPTER II

BEYOND THE TRADITIONAL FEMININE ROLE

'Who Would Be Free, Herself Must Strike The Blow'
(Caption on a poster for the National Union of Women Teachers)

The First World War opened out new opportunities and altered conditions for women, which brought in turn gradual acknowledgement of the right – and the need – for women to move from the private to the public sphere of activity. Yet it was a great cultural leap and understanding its implications took a long time, the old and the new expectations often co-existing.

Medical care and nursing in particular was a perfect example. The role of women in caring for the sick is an ancient one and, until the great medical developments of the mid-twentieth century, most women of all social classes would expect to be involved with it in their domestic life. Because it was so acceptable a part of the traditional image, it was easier for the public imagination to respond without difficulty to women as they extended this role at the outbreak of war, and possibly for this reason there are so many official photographs of them. This had been reinforced also by the example of a remarkable Victorian woman, Florence Nightingale, who had made nursing a respectable occupation for women. She had also given the nursing profession its uniform, which echoed the habit of the religious orders – the only traditional image of the selfless woman dedicated to an ideal outside the home and family circle. By 1914 nursing and its uniform was generally accepted as a public commitment to a private (that is, non-state) professional duty. As many of the photographs show, women in this romanticised role were not perceived as a threat to the standard notions of womanhood.

The British Army was a small, highly mobile, self-sufficient force and, like the rest of Europe, quite unprepared for the strain on its resources caused by the unprecedented number of war wounded. The Army nursing services were small, although since 1910 they had been supplemented by the War Office Scheme for Voluntary Aid Detachments to the Sick and Wounded (hence VAD). This offered one of the earliest routes to war service for girls from middle- and upper-class backgrounds; they had to be financially self-sufficient or supported by their families as they were, of course, unpaid. This frequently caused problems between the amateurs and the professionals: the latter resented the need to train raw recruits who were also likely to come from different social backgrounds. This and the often poor conditions added to the increasing stress on young VADs expected to deal with the horrific mutilations of war for which their First Aid courses had scarcely prepared them. The shock of the experience is vividly described in the memoirs of two of the most famous VADs, Vera Brittain and Lady Diana Manners.

Yet, in spite of all this, the work of the VADs had offered women their chance to participate in the great events of the day, an opportunity which they had never had before. As the many men volunteering for war service gave women the chance of change, travel and adventure, and in fact prepared society for wider alterations in the image of women, it was not surprising that those few women already leading successful professional careers would pioneer this. They were used to working in an almost wholly male-dominated professional environment and they took the initiative early on. The Women's Hospital Corps, the Scottish Women's Hospitals and individual units like that of the Women of Pervyse took the lead not only in organising and running superb medical units but in moving these towards the battlefield itself. Not surprisingly, the male officers and civil servants at the top of the military hierarchy were Victorian in outlook and found it difficult dealing with women on a professional basis. It was perhaps inevitable that the most clear-cut clash in the long-running dispute over equal pay should emerge in the medical field involving highly experienced women whose professional skills were at a premium. Thus the popular notion of the pretty plucky VAD succouring the wounded hero is counterpointed by the powerful concept of the skilled woman who possessed the unfeminine attributes of knowledge, efficiency and coolness in emotionally trying circumstances. As tales of the exploits of the women serving abroad and the dangers they ran began to filter back home another element was added: bravery.

This was underlined by the awarding of military honours to women. Just as the public need for a hero had been met by Rupert Brooke, so the change in the perception of women is crystallised by the corresponding need for a heroine: Edith Cavell. In assimilating the masculine virtues of courage and sacrifice in war to the 'feminine' ones of gentleness and care for the sick, she brought a positive strength and excitement to the image of women. All women who wanted to participate in the war effort now had to learn to organise themselves, as they had no tradition of being organised. All over the country groups and committees were springing up to support the war effort and relieve distress at home. In addition to comforts for the troops ('Sister Susie sewing shirts for soldiers' in the words of a popular song), they turned their attention to assisting the interests of women at all levels: nationally like Queen Mary, Mary Macarthur and Margaret Bondfield with the Central Committee for Women's Training and Employment, and locally like the Women's Emergency Corps with its work-rooms for women in different London boroughs. In fact it was the very lack of an official relationship with the state that gave women in the early part of the war a scope and freedom they were seldom to enjoy again. Although the Defence of the Realm Act, 1914 (popularly known as DORA), had started to change everyday life by introducing a hitherto unknown measure of state control – licensing laws, censorship of news – much of the early civilian war effort depended entirely on private fund-raising and voluntary work. Women were by far the most experienced in this field.

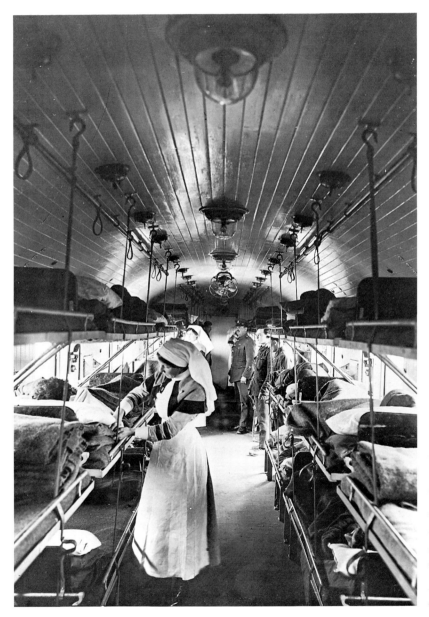

PLATE 16
Interior of a ward on a British Ambulance Train, near Doullens, 27 April 1918

Care of the sick was an ancient female skill, and before modern medical developments, women of all social classes could expect to be involved in looking after their families' illnesses. So familiarity made nurses acceptable in the male domain of the battlefield to both military and civilian alike. The difficulty of constantly moving large numbers of wounded men behind the lines is apparent in this photograph, and the skills of female nurses became essential to it.

Photographer: Unknown
Source: IWM Q8749

PLATE 17
Interior view of the Princess Victoria Rest Club for Nurses, Etaples, 7 November 1917

That remarkable Victorian, Florence Nightingale, had transformed nursing into a respectable occupation for women, and uniquely, one where it was possible for women to make a public commitment to a private (that is, a non-state) professional duty. The distinctive uniform, which she instigated, was a visible symbol of this. More importantly for the 1914 generation she also set the only official precedent for women's involvement close to front-line warfare. Both nurses and female medical staff reached Belgium and France in the autumn of 1914 and by 1917 were well established there.

Photographer: Unknown
Source: IWM Q3170

PLATE 18 *Above*

Competitors arriving for a fishing contest between the nurses of hospital barges, Watten, 8 June 1918

For women at this time the adoption of a uniform became a sign of sought-after professional status, as well as of patriotic dedication. The uniforms of the Army nursing services managed to combine the traditional and familiar nursing elements of starched cotton and nun-like coif with the smart and distinctive practicality of military dress. These two nursing sisters, whose uniforms were grey with scarlet facings, were members of the Territorial Force Nursing Service. The all-scarlet cape, or 'Tippet' was reserved for members of the Queen Alexandra's Imperial Military Nursing Service. The TFNS, founded in 1908 as a result of the Haldane Reforms, which saw the establishment of the Territorial Army, provided by far and away the largest number of nursing sisters serving with the armies at home and abroad.

Photographer: Unknown *Source:* IWM Q8892

PLATE 19 *Opposite, above*

Fishing contest between nurses of hospital barges, Watten, 8 June 1918

The pastoral tranquillity of this scene reveals the photographer responding to the broad Flemish countryside much as traditional landscape painters had done. He reveals a similar tendency to be influenced by his Victorian artist predecessors in romanticising these nurses, here seemingly safely removed from the mess and strain of the casualty station. In reality these serene barges were floating wards, and the calm canals busy with military traffic.

Photographer: Unknown *Source:* IWM Q8895

PLATE 20 *Left*
Deck of a hospital barge showing four nursing sisters and a Royal Army Medical Corps Captain, near Aire, 14 September 1918

It is not surprising that the only women's organisations officially recognised by the military authorities in 1914 were the Army nursing services, founded on the recommendation of a Royal Commission following the Boer War. The services, both Regular and Territorial, adopted the relatively modern principle of promotion on merit rather than seniority. The Army nursing services grew from just over 3,000 members in 1914 to over 23,000 by 1918.

Photographer: Unknown
Source: IWM Q106688

PLATE 21
Dr Patterson and Miss North at work in the laboratory, 25 Stationary Hospital, Rouen

The unprecedented casualties of modern warfare over-strained the existing military medical services, to which charitable volunteer help became essential. While some VADs were men, the majority were women, especially the nurses. Female VAD numbers rose from 47,196 on 1 August 1914 to 82,857 by April 1920. Their acceptability to the military authorities and the public sprang not only from the traditional aspects of nursing discussed earlier, but also from the fact that their working relations with men were a continuation of those in civilian medical life: the male doctor is in charge of the assisting nurse. What the image also incidentally makes clear is that nursing was an activity demanding 'unfeminine' skills of precision, efficiency and coolness in emotionally trying circumstances.

Photographer: Unknown
Source: IWM Q108212

PLATE 22
The Prince of Wales at the Duchess of Sutherland's Hospital at Calais during a visit by the King and Queen, 14 June 1917

The reality behind the romantic popular image of the VAD was very different. They were of course unpaid, which meant that recruits tended to be drawn from women who could finance themselves, like two famous VADs, Vera Brittain and Lady Diana Manners. The nurses shown here with the Prince are clearly, from their relaxed posture, socially at ease with him and likely to be themselves upper class. Class differences in fact exacerbated the problem many VADs encountered with the professional nurses under whom they worked, who disliked training the inexperienced and also resented the manifestation of different class attitudes and means. Yet the VADs too were frequently exploited; they worked amazingly hard in inadequate conditions while despised by some of the professionals as incompetent 'do-gooders'.

Photographer: Unknown
Source: IWM Q2585

PLATE 24 *Opposite, above*
German ward of 4 Stationary Hospital, Longuenesse

By August 1918 there were over 8,000 nurses and female orderlies, drivers and other medical staff working in France alone. Yet in spite of the response from women, the voluntary system from 1916 onwards was proving inadequate to cope with the casualties. The military authorities introduced payment of £20–£30 per annum to VADs, hence conflicting with the neutral status of the charitable bodies which is here underlined by their nursing of German wounded. It provoked the leaders of the women's organisations into demanding officially constituted bodies of women to be paid by the Government.

Photographer: Unknown
Source: IWM Q108203

PLATE 25 *Opposite, below*
A German prisoner having his wounded hand dressed in the VAD dressing station at Abbéville with his escort, 27 June 1917

The dressing stations provided immediate emergency medical aid for the wounded after which the serious cases would be sent down the line to the hospital. This would be as close to the front lines as any woman with the British Expeditionary Force would get. Here the basic nature of the medical resources is apparent.

Photographer: Unknown
Source: IWM Q2469

PLATE 26
Dame Maud McCarthy, Matron-in-Chief of Queen Alexandra's Imperial Military Nursing Service with the British Armies in France, in her office at Boulogne Headquarters, c. 1918

By the second half of the war the women's organisations had grown beyond all expectation and their leaders, such as Dame Maud (Dame Ethel Becher ran the organisation at home), were running large and complex administrations often under very difficult conditions. Dame Maud's grey and scarlet uniform dress, with its elaborate frogging on the bodice, recalls not only the pre-war splendour of military full dress, but emphasises the very special status of the QAIMNS as part of the military establishment. It had been a small and exclusive corps before the First World War, and it would revert to that again when the war finished.

Photographer: Unknown
Source: IWM Q108193

PLATE 27
**TFNS nursing sister talking to a wounded soldier by a hospital train at
Dernacourt, September 1916**

Nurses were the only women, from their own nations, that many soldiers
were likely to meet on active service; while the majority of Army nurses were
British, there were Australians, New Zealanders, Canadians, South Africans
and Americans among the VADs. It was expected of the nurses that they
maintain a professional distance from their patients (and the male medical
staff) while responding to the natural human desire to alleviate the bleak
circumstances with a little human contact, as here. War also brought an
upheaval in the settled moral codes of the nineteenth century, to the confusion
of the authorities, both male and female, who constantly tried to impose
complete social segregation, which became unworkable. Many women,
especially those from sheltered backgrounds, record too the shock of
discovering that different classes had very different notions of what
constituted acceptable or unacceptable behaviour.

Photographer: Unknown
Source: IWM Q1319

PLATE 28
Patients playing cards outside the Australian Hospital, Mudros: three nurses looking on

For the first time women's services were officially needed on the battlefields beyond the Western Front, in the Balkans and the Eastern Mediterranean. There may well be Australian VADs with this group of Australian and British soldiers in this typical field hospital under canvas.
The onlooker reading the *Sydney Mail* is possibly making a point about 'down-under'. It also perhaps shows how unused were that generation to the camera.

Photographer: Unknown
Source: IWM Q13720

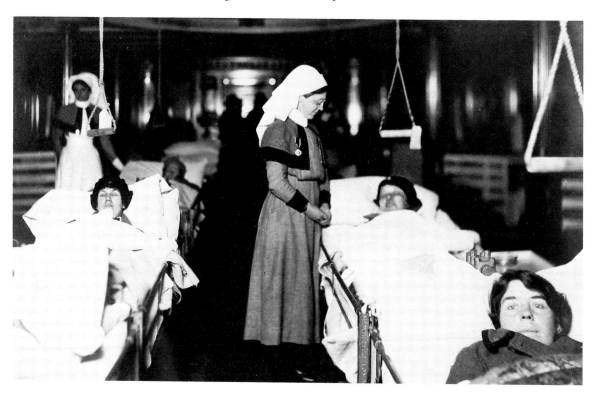

PLATE 29 *Over, top left*
Army nurses and VADs being nursed aboard the hospital ship *St Andrew*

Although not in the front line, women working close to the battlefields, or as here involved in shipping the sick and wounded from the Western Front and Eastern Mediterranean to Britain, became increasingly vulnerable to attack, and in the Balkan theatre to infections such as typhus. The exact number of casualties is not known, but numbers of women succumbed to illness, and members of the nursing services were lost with hospital ships sunk as a result of enemy action. This is an unusual picture of women patients being cared for by members of the Army nursing services, and the relative rarity of such images suggests that the authorities, ever concerned about the morale of those in or out of uniform, did not wish to over-emphasise this aspect of women's war work.

Photographer: Unknown
Source: IWM Q108222

PLATE 30 *Over, bottom left*
Damage done during the air raids on the Hospital Area, Etaples, 2 June 1918: 9 Canadian Stationary Hospital bombed on the night of 31 May

Although still in its infancy, the air raid was a new and terrible weapon which from June 1915 also began to affect the hitherto immune Home Front, when Zeppelin and aircraft attacks caused approximately 5,000 casualties, many of them women and children. It is unusual at this period to find an image such as this which catches something of the immediacy and shock of the event.

Photographer: Thomas K. Aitken
Source: IWM Q11541

PLATE 31 *Over, right*
Funeral of a nursing sister killed during the bombing of Etaples, 3 June 1918

The death of women, especially nurses, when carefully presented to the public, as in this case, could prove a strong propaganda weapon. The image of the military funeral with its rather theatrical formality is uplifting and dignified and removes the humdrum mess and pain in a way that the image of women wounded and sick does not.

Photographer: Thomas K. Aitken
Source: IWM Q11034

PLATE 32 *Opposite*
Edith Cavell (1865–1915) with her dogs

Edith Cavell, the daughter of a Norfolk clergyman, became the first nationally acclaimed heroine and female martyr of the war. As such she had a significant effect on popular perceptions of the role of women and made it central to the British war propaganda effort. A professional nurse of long standing, Edith Cavell had already pursued a successful career, and in 1914, when war broke out, she was the Directrice of a School of Nursing in the Belgian capital, Brussels. A woman of deeply held Christian beliefs and of the principle that

as a nurse it was her duty to aid the sick and wounded, friend or foe, she nonetheless took the decision actively to assist in the escape of Allied soldiers caught behind the German lines when the BEF made its retreat from Mons. This decision brought her into direct contravention of German military law then in force in Brussels. She was arrested, tried by a German Military Court, found guilty and shot. It is arguable that the Germans were well within their rights to exact the supreme penalty from her, but they would have been wiser to have locked her up for the duration, because her death was a gift to the Allies who presented her as the brave and innocent victim of Prussian barbarism. This of course capitalised on the traditional 'feminine' aura surrounding the nurse while infusing a new element, the hitherto 'masculine' qualities of direct public action and courage in a patriotic cause. It is worth noting that Edith Cavell is remembered in her own country for the circumstances and manner of her death; in Belgium she is remembered as one of the founders of that country's modern nursing services.

Photographer: Unknown
Source: IWM Q32930

PLATE 33
The Baroness de T'Serclaes and Miss Mairi Chisholm attending to a wounded soldier in a street at Ramscapelle, 11 September 1917

Mairi Chisholm was 18 when she left her aristocratic Scottish family, against her mother's wishes, riding down to London on her newly acquired motorbike to join the war effort. By way of despatch riding for the Women's Emergency Corps and then driving for an ambulance group in Belgium, she joined forces with an experienced nurse, Elsie Knocker, who later married a Belgian officer, the Baron de T'Serclaes. They set up a First Aid Post at the front in the Belgian sector, the only women to work virtually in the front lines, and remained there until they were both gassed early in 1918. Known simply as 'the Women of Pervyse' they were each awarded the Belgian Order of Leopold and the Military Medal. Mairi, who drove the ambulance, is on the right; the screens in the background are camouflage for the road.

Photographer: Unknown
Source: IWM Q2963

PLATE 34
Sergeant-Major Flora Sandes, Salonika, January 1917

Flora Sandes was the daughter of a Suffolk clergyman who, at the age of 38, went to Serbia as a nurse with a Red Cross ambulance unit. Caught up in the terrible retreat into Albania, she became separated from her unit and attached herself to a Serbian regiment, taking the oath of allegiance for convenience and safety. She rose through the ranks to become a Sergeant-Major and after being seriously wounded in the 1916 Serbian advance on Monastir was awarded the Order of Karageorge. As a Lieutenant she remained on active service until 1922, then married a Russian émigré officer and remained in Belgrade until 1945, having spent the second war interned by the Germans. When widowed she returned to Suffolk, where she lived quietly until her death in 1961. She is shown here in her Serbian Army uniform, wearing her Order of Karageorge. Flora Sandes was the only British woman to enrol officially as a soldier in the First World War and the only one known to have borne arms against the enemy.

Photographer: Unknown
Source: IWM Q32702

PLATE 35
Dr Elsie Maud Inglis (1865–1917)

Dr Elsie Inglis, founder of the Scottish Women's Hospitals, was one of the first women doctors to have studied in Edinburgh under the pioneer Dr Sophia Jex Blake, and worked in London with two others, Dr Elizabeth Garrett Anderson and her daughter Louisa. Not surprisingly she was also a leader of the Scottish NUWSS and by 1914 had settled into an active medical career. When war was declared she proposed to the Scottish Suffrage Societies the staffing, funding and equipping of an all-woman medical unit to offer to the military authorities. When in a famous phrase the latter told her to 'Go home and sit still' she organised her units and offered them to the Allies. By the end of the war there were fourteen Scottish Women's Hospital units attached to virtually every Allied Force – except the British. Elsie Inglis herself went as overall administrator to Serbia in 1915, where much of the most famous and demanding work was done. Taken prisoner-of-war with her staff, she was repatriated in 1916 and took another unit to Russia. Caught up in the Russian Revolution, they were evacuated in November 1917 by the Royal Navy, and Dr Inglis died at Newcastle the day after their return; thousands attended her funeral in Edinburgh. She is shown here in the SWH uniform which she designed.
Photographer: Unknown
Source: IWM Q68949A

PLATE 36
**Dr G. Eleanor Soltau, Chief Medical Officer at
Kragujevac, on her return to Britain from Serbia**

Dr Soltau was in charge of the first Scottish Women's
Hospital Unit to be sent to Kragujevac, northern Serbia,
in January 1915. Fully equipped for 100 patients, they
were coping by the spring with 650. Instead of war
wounded, this unit and others found themselves treating
a typhus epidemic. Three women of the unit died of the
infection during the severe winter, and after pulling her
patients and staff through the worst, Dr Soltau, who had
worked throughout her own bout of diphtheria, had to
be invalided home later in the year. She is wearing here
the Serbian Order of St Sava and the Serbian Order of
the Red Cross and her hair (touched up in the original
photograph) is growing out from being cropped against
the fever.
Photographer: Unknown
Source: IWM Q10814

PLATE 37
Dr Beatrice McGregor and Miss Pares, Serbia

Dr McGregor and Miss Pares were the Chief Medical Officer and Administrator respectively of an SWH unit
stationed first at Mladenovac on the Austrian border. Driven southwards by the Austrian invasion to
Kragujevac with other medical units, and carrying their wounded with them, they set up a huge dressing
station there and dealt in two weeks with 10,000 Serbian casualties. In consultation with Dr Inglis (see plate
35) most units decided to remain to care for the wounded and await the enemy. Others, including Dr McGregor
and Miss Pares, chose to accompany the Serbian army and the thousands of refugees in the retreat across
the Albanian mountains into Greece.
Photographer: Unknown
Source: IWM Q108187

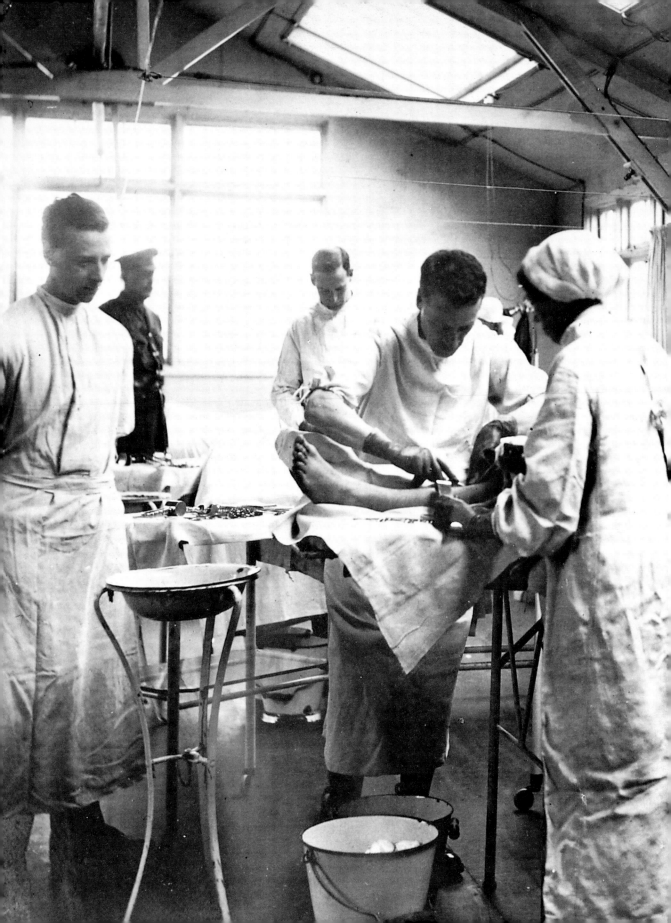

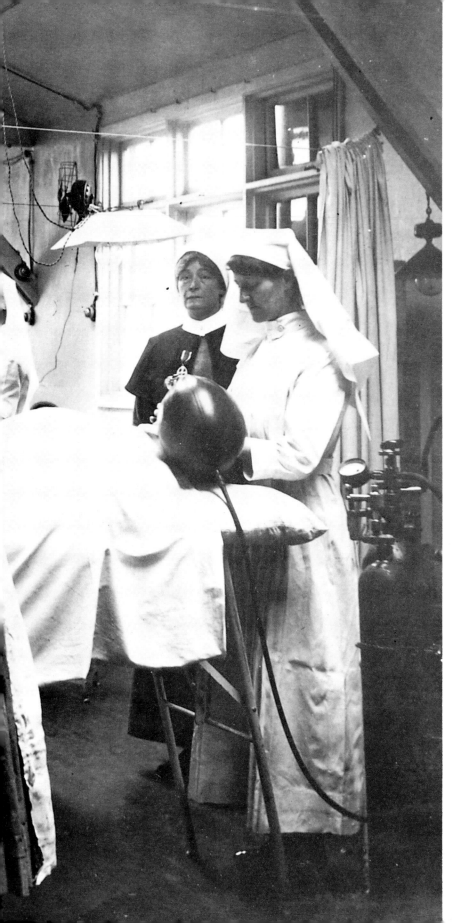

PLATE 38
No. 32 Stationary Hospital at Wimereux, operating theatre: Colonel Fullerton conducting an operation

Here the male surgeon is being assisted by a female medical officer. In addition to women doctors and surgeons employed by the regular Red Cross hospitals there were also the units established and run by female medical staff, like the one administered by the former suffragette Dr Louisa Garrett Anderson and Dr Flora Murray and entirely staffed by women at Wimereux. This and the formidable SWH units were funded from Britain by committees of the various women's groups, and female communities all over Britain raised and supported their own: the women's colleges at Cambridge, for instance.

Photographer: Unknown
Source: IWM Q108192

PLATE 39
Members of the First Aid Nursing Yeomanry serving as ambulance drivers with the Belgian Army, Calais, 8 May 1918

The First Aid Nursing Yeomanry, known as the FANY, was founded in 1907 as a mounted nursing corps to bring wounded in from the battlefield, though they never actually performed this somewhat Valkyrie-like role. However, as Mairi Chisholm had shown at Pervyse, the work of the ambulance drivers was difficult, dangerous and vital. Driving skills were not, of course, widespread amongst the population at this period, but motor transport of all kinds became more and more important as the war progressed, and was an area where women increasingly took over from men. As the horse gave way to the motor vehicle so the FANYs adapted themselves to their new role of drivers instead of riders.

Photographer: Unknown
Source: IWM Q3257

PLATE 40
Mabel Ann Stobart Greenhalgh (known always as Mrs St Clair Stobart)

The daughter of a well-to-do county family, 50 years old when war broke out, twice married and widely travelled, Mabel St Clair Stobart belonged to that succession of intrepid Victorian and Edwardian ladies who benefited from the confidence of their class and independent means, and whose forceful personalities could therefore find expression in defying the limitations placed on their more conventional sisters. In the Bulgarian War with Turkey in 1912 she had already led a female medical unit, and at home was interested in women's suffrage activity. In 1914 she immediately formed a similar Women's Sick and Wounded Convoy Corps to serve with the Belgian Army, and her experience made her an obvious choice to do the same in Serbia for the Serbian Relief Fund. When the Austrians invaded Serbia in 1914 she agreed to Serbian requests to lead a flying field hospital to the front lines, and she and her staff were caught up, like so many of the women's medical units, in the terrible Serbian retreat across the Albanian mountains. Her imperious nature brought her into conflict with her own staff and the Serbian Relief Fund administration back in Britain. Like another pioneering Serbian Relief organiser, Leila Lady Paget, she found that the Britain of 1917 to which she returned had changed; there was no room for the high-handed decisions made without reference to others that had characterised their driving force in the less organised early days. Mrs St Clair Stobart retired from active war work.

Photographer: Unknown
Source: IWM Q69129

PLATE 41
FANY ambulance drivers in their fur coats, Calais, January 1917

The FANY were mostly upper-class women and brought to their work a sense of *ésprit de corps* often borrowed from their brothers serving as officers in the Army. Their dashing image, something which they rather prided themselves on, can be seen to be well established by the splendid fur coats worn over their khaki uniforms. By August 1918 there were 116 FANYs working in France under the auspices of the Red Cross.

Photographer: Unknown
Source: IWM Q4673

PLATE 42 *Above*
**VAD drivers of the convoy
attached to 814 Mechanical
Transport Company,
Boulogne, attending to the
maintenance of their cars,
1 September 1918**

While only upper-class
women were likely to have
had the opportunity of
learning to drive on a father's
or brother's car, women
whose family occupations
brought them into contact
with motor transport would
also learn. Many blacksmiths,
for example, had already
added car maintenance to
shoeing horses, and their
womenfolk would help with
both. After 1918 women did
not relinquish the driving
skills which were gradually to
offer them unprecedented
mobility and freedom as the
century progressed.

Photographer: Unknown
Source: IWM Q9292

PLATE 44
Mrs McDougal, Organising Officer of the FANY

The FANY was the only pre-war voluntary women's group to survive two world wars and flourish today as the Women's Transport Service (FANY). It became one of the most famous women's wartime units, particularly in the Second World War. The First World War underpinned their amateur dash with professional competence. They left nursing to other groups and developed specialised skills, enlarging their reputation as an élite group. The professionalism shows in Mrs MacDougal's crisply military uniform: the élite style in the silk cravat held by a jewelled pin.

Photographer: Unknown
Source: IWM Q107972

PLATE 43 *Left*
Member of the Women's Hospital Corps, Endell Street, *c.* 1918

The Women's Hospital Corps was one of the first wartime groups, formed by September 1914 in France, complete with the uniform here shown of grey-green, the hat trimmed with a green veil. As with the SWH, it was the medical women already leading successful civilian careers who early on established some of the most efficient medical units close to the battle zones. So high was their reputation that Dr Flora Murray and Dr Louisa Garrett Anderson were asked to return to London and run an entire military hospital at Endell Street. This they did throughout the war, staffing it from surgeons to orderlies entirely with women. Flora Murray, although appointed surgeon-in-charge, was denied the official rank of Lieutenant-Colonel which would have been held by a male surgeon.

Photographer: Horace W. Nicholls
Source: IWM Q30617

PLATE 45
Dr Dorothy Hare, Assistant Medical Director, Women's Royal Naval Service,
c. **1918**

By 1916 the voluntary organisations which had resourcefully filled the many
breaches in the official war effort were evidently no longer enough; the
military authorities were already recognising the need for a regular paid body
of women officially funded and administered. The heads of the major women's
organisations suspected this but wanted such a body to be run by women;
military views had not yet caught up with changing circumstances. For
instance, the male organisations employing VAD nurses and drivers refused
to let the appropriate voluntary body such as the Red Cross oversee their
welfare and conditions. As was all too apparent on the Home Front, squalid
and dirty conditions of work were regarded as normal; it was the increasing
employment of women that forced change. The women had their way when
the Women's Services were formed. Dame Katherine Furse, Commandant of
the VADs, was made Director WRNS in 1917 with female staff, such as Dr
Hare pictured here. The aim of busy efficiency is apparent in the desk
paraphernalia of paper and telephone; characteristic of the women's offices
generally are the vases of flowers.

Photographer: Unknown
Source: IWM Q19705

PLATE 46
**The Women's Royal Air Force in France in the persons of Dr Lily Baker,
Honorary Medical Officer In Charge WRAF in the Field (*left*) and Miss
Chauncey (*right*), Maresquel, April 1919**

It was the women doctors, who were formed into an Auxiliary Corps of the
RAMC like these WRAF Medical Officers, who fought for and achieved equal
pay with the men (though not comparable rank and allowances). The War
Office was astonished and indignant to find that female doctors commanding
high incomes in civilian life refused to accept less than their male counterparts
from the military authorities simply because they were women. It was a single
but significant victory.

Photographer: Unknown
Source: IWM Q3762

PLATE 47
Member of Glasgow Battalion of the Women's Volunteer Reserve at a canteen for soldiers and civilians *c.* 1915

The WVR aimed to provide 'a trained and efficient body of women whose services could be offered to the country at any time' (WVR pamphlet). As early as December 1914 a Member of Parliament was stressing that women in uniform did not imply the bearing of arms by women, revealing how disturbing was that notion. Many of the duties of the WVR and the later bodies modelled on it were identical to the domestic ones they undertook in their private lives.

Photographer: Unknown   *Source:* IWM Q107998

CHAPTER III

FROM RESPONSE TO INITIATIVE

'Women Demand the Right to Serve'
(Women's Right to Serve, March 1915)

The declaration of war in August 1914 had a remarkable effect, at least for a time, on the various discordant factions of pre-war Britain. Political parties, trade unions, the Irish and the suffragettes saw the war as a transcendent cause to unify and direct their energies against a common enemy. On 5 August Decima Moore and the Hon. Evelina Haverfield, the latter an aristocratic and militant suffragette, decided that here was an opportunity women must seize and they formed the Women's Emergency Corps. They were joined not only by other feminists like Mrs Pethick Lawrence, but also by women who would not normally associate with the suffragettes, like the Duchess of Sutherland and the Marchioness of Londonderry. Further, it was made clear that the WEC was both non-political and non-sectarian; yet its aim was impeccably feminist. This was to provide women as paid, not voluntary, helpers. As the WEC's First Annual Report stated, the object was to organise '... women's help in the national crises, to deal effectively and promptly with whatever emergencies might arise' (WEC, First Annual Report 1914/15, IWM Women's Work Collection Volunteer Corps 1.1.1/29).

In time of war the course of action became for men quite simple and straightforward: the state summoned them and organised them. Women had no such clear path to follow and no role model except in fact that offered by the men: the Armed Services. The direct result of this was that almost without exception the early women's organisations adopted quasi-military uniform, a chain of command and rank structures, the clear implication being that they too were soldiers ready and willing to fight a common foe. The two most important of these were the Women's Volunteer Reserve and the Women's Legion which both developed directly out of the WEC, and paved the way for all the similar organisations for women which were to follow. They fulfilled a real need not only by employing women, but in directing much of their work towards care for the interests of women as a whole. A good example of this is the work of the women police groups, which not only offered jobs to unemployed women but also held as their main aim the protection of women and girls both in the factories and on the streets.

The leaders of the suffragettes and suffragists took very different directions as the war progressed. As previously indicated, the NUWSS led by Millicent Garrett Fawcett was involved in practical war work by and for women, whilst maintaining a watching brief over women's interests. It continued to make representations to the Government on all matters affecting women, and never lost sight of its original political aim: women's suffrage. Emmeline Pankhurst and her daughter Christabel of the WSPU, on the other hand, took a very different view of the opportunities that war offered women. They aimed to show that in patriotic endeavour women were the equal of men. They replaced the suffragette slogan 'Votes for Women' with 'For King, for Country, for Freedom'. This change of attitude shocked many of their former supporters, who saw as ironical this enthusiastic endorsement of the establishment they had so strenuously fought in the past. The sense of disquiet was further compounded by the Pankhursts' new and public commitment to recruiting for the Armed Services. Some feminists in fact refused to involve themselves at all in the war effort, believing pacifism to be inherent in feminism. Suffragists and suffragettes together shared this view, both being prominent for example in the No-Conscription Fellowship founded in December 1914. Sylvia Pankhurst also renounced publicly her family's endorsement of the war effort. She devoted herself to alleviating the hardships produced among the lower classes by economic uncertainty and disruption. While keeping the interests of women in view, she widened the scope of her efforts to include the rights of disadvantaged men. To emphasise the latter she changed the name of 'The East London Federation', her branch of the WSPU, to 'The Workers' Suffrage Federation'. Mary Macarthur and Margaret Bondfield, already veterans of the women's trade unions and the Labour movement, continued to develop their political activities on behalf of women. Both would find that their wartime experience gave them an impetus to continue tackling some of these problems affecting women and children when the war was over. In this they were typical of many women whose abilities were first given fuller scope by the war.

PLATE 48
Type of uniform worn by officer and private, Women's Volunteer Reserve

War brought together women who would not normally have associated with each other, like the radical suffragette and the conservative aristocrat. Both found that the state offered men a straightforward course to follow, but ignored women, so they organised a role for themselves. From the earliest body, the Women's Emergency Corps of August 1914, developed the Women's Volunteer Reserve, led by the remarkable suffragette the Hon. Evelina Haverfield. The khaki coat, skirt and felt hat, with shoes and puttees, cost £2.10s – beyond the reach of lower-class women.

Photographer: Horace W. Nicholls
Source: IWM Q30344

PLATE 49
Lady Major Egger of The Lady Instructors' Signals Company, *c.* 1918

This interesting little group, started in 1914, was set up by yet another, the Women's Emergency League, to operate in the Aldershot Command, Aldershot in Hampshire, then, as now, the 'Home' of the British Army, and it seems that these two women's groups, like so many, were local ones catering to local needs. In this case the Lady Signallers were an example of early co-operation with the Army, and here not on the usual level of simply providing domestic services. Throughout the war they trained army cadets in signalling skills.

Photographer: Horace W. Nicholls
Source: IWM Q30623

PLATE 50
**Lannock Summer Camp
1916: a transmitting station**

Once the WVR and the other
organisations had led the
way, most middle- and upper-
class women especially
embraced the concept of
uniting as a group of women
and adopting uniform. Far
from seeing it as disturbing,
women took it as a badge of
patriotic service and of a
public role (albeit an
unofficial one) which was at
last accessible to women.
Many small regional groups
such as this Signallers' Corps
were founded: they mostly
learnt such skills as
signalling, First Aid and camp
cooking, rather as their
daughters did in the Girl
Guides.

Photographer: Unknown
Source: IWM Q108031

Plate 51
Women's Legion: a member of the Agricultural Section, *c.* **1918**

During the late nineteenth century British agriculture was in decline; low wages forced men and women off the land to other occupations. The war revitalised the need for the home production of food and for some home labour. From small beginnings, providing seasonal help with fruit picking, grew the women's agricultural groups initiated by the Women's Board at the Board of Agriculture and Fisheries. Represented on this for the first time were women's labour organisations such as the NUWW, who appointed female inspectors to oversee recruitment, medical welfare, accommodation and training. The earliest group was the Women's Forage Corps of 1915 (to find fodder for horses). The two major bodies, the Women's Land Army and the Women's Forestry Corps, started in 1917. As with the other official organisations, proper pay meant that working women could afford to join; many came to the land from the munitions factories, seeking a healthier occupation.

Photographer: Horace W. Nicholls
Source: IWM Q30385

PLATE 52
Women's Auxiliary Force: Highbury Branch members working on their allotment, *c*. 1915

The Women's Auxiliary Force was founded in 1915 by the Misses Walthall and Sparshott to organise employment specifically for part-time workers. In addition to the usual drill, first aid, cooking and sewing, the WAF, like most of the voluntary groups, specialised in particular areas; they provided canteens and set up and administered clubs for the entertaining of troops; they acted as stewards in air-raid shelters and as well as regular hospital visiting they grew vegetables for hospitals, as here at Highbury. Their uniform has the characteristic elaboration of the early part of the war: it was blue with khaki facings.

Photographer: Unknown
Source: IWM Q108033

PLATE 53
Procession of women demanding the right to enter the war services, London, Saturday 17 July 1915

In spite of the considerable achievement of women's voluntary work, women, after a year of war effort, were still largely ignored by the state. The first great opportunity to assert women's rights to a new relationship with government, industry and trade unions came with the revelation of a serious shell shortage in 1915. The new Minister of Munitions, David Lloyd George, who had often skirmished with Mrs Pankhurst in the past, now with characteristic astuteness enlisted her formidable aid in a propaganda drive to convince both women and employers of the need for female labour on a large scale. With a grant of some £3,000 from the Ministry, Mrs Pankhurst and the WSPU organised the last of the famous suffragette marches. Instead of the vote, the aim was access to industrial jobs, especially munitions; now the banners were proclaiming: 'Women Demand the Right to Serve'.

Photographer: Unknown
Source: IWM Q105767

PLATE 54
Women's Legion: a member of the Canteen Section, *c.* 1918

The Women's Legion was launched by the Marchioness of Londonderry in July 1915 and became the most widespread and successful of the voluntary organisations, with tens of thousands of members by 1917. As this suggests, the WL had managed to enlarge its appeal beyond the middle and upper classes as the WVR, of which Lady Londonderry was an early leader, had not. Lady Londonderry began to realise that the 'officer and gentleman' ethos of the WVR and similar groups was alien to the large numbers of women now seeking work, and her new organisation was less military in style. It still had a uniform and 'officers', but its specialisations reflected the familiar unmilitary world, although it provided services for the Army. Biggest of these were the Military Cooking Section, the Canteen Section and the Agricultural Section, and accommodation and training were provided also for its members. Its success convinced the authorities that an official military unit for women would be workable.

Photographer: Horace W. Nicholls
Source: IWM Q30347

PLATE 55
Women's Police Patrol collaborating with a constable outside Euston Station

The patrols carried authorisation cards and their main duties lay where troops gathered, and therefore, women and girls also. Then as now, railway stations, like Euston, were such areas. Although not yet officially linked with the Metropolitan Police, they regularly liaised with them. Known also as the Voluntary Women's Patrols (VWP) they were expected to perform a two-hour period of garrison duty on at least two days a week; in towns they were full-time.

Photographers: Unknown
Source: IWM Q31088

PLATE 56
Women's Police Patrols with soldiers at a London railway station, *c.* **1916**

The Women's Police Patrols formed the first of two female police groups; inaugurated in September 1914 by the National Union of Women Workers, its duties were to patrol round military camps and shore stations to protect women and girls. The NUWW had been in favour of a women's police force for some time; for just as women of the more privileged classes saw it as a religious and social duty to safeguard the moral welfare of their less fortunate sisters, so also did the leaders of the women's trade union movement. Indeed saving vulnerable women and children from exploitation was a great part of their ultimate aim, and modern sensitivity to this as patronising would not have occurred to them. The Women's Police Patrols were a good example of this unselfconscious practical morality in action.

Photographer: Unknown

PLATE 57
Mrs Theo Stanley, Superior of Special Women's Patrols

The success of the Voluntary Women's Police Patrols led to the recognition by the authorities of their usefulness. In 1916 the Commissioner of the Metropolitan Police directly employed thirty patrols under Mrs Theo Stanley. By 1917 their work was made full-time. Not only was the job one where women were dealing with their own sex, as the pre-war women's movement had demanded, but it was also creating employment for women thrown out of work by the upheaval of the wartime economy. It was something of a triumph for the NUWW, whose armband Mrs Stanley still wears.

Photographer: Unknown
Source: IWM Q108496

PLATE 58
Margaret Damer Dawson OBE (*left*), **Commandant of the Women's Police Service, with the Sub-Commandant Mary S. Allen OBE,** *c.* 1917

The Women's Police Service also originated with a pre-war women's suffrage group, the Women's Freedom League, to which one of its founders, Miss Nina Boyle, belonged. Her co-founder was Margaret Damer Dawson, who became Commandant. The first two uniformed officers, including Mary Allen, were employed in November 1914 at the Grantham military camp, to be followed by Edith Smith, often described as the first policewoman. After 1916 they tended to work in and around the multiplying munitions factories which were increasing their female employees. The various women's police groups (all superseded in 1918 by the official Metropolitan Police Women Patrols under Mrs Stanley) represented a first step towards the professional rather than charitable engagement of women in social welfare, as well as law and order.

Photographer: Unknown
Source: IWM Q108495

PLATE 59
Nurses tending a slight casualty in a shell filling factory, *c.* 1917

The need for reform of bad working conditions was intensified by female labour. As so often, resistance gave before the twin pressures of morality and hygiene: the irrefutable need for separate – and clean – lavatory facilities for instance, often where scarcely any facilities at all existed before. The new propaganda effort of which these photographs were a part was double-edged: the Government found that applauding the courage of munitionettes undertaking dangerous work also focussed public attention on existing conditions. Medical services as well as canteens had to be provided – and as here these were also largely staffed by women. The Ministry of Munitions established a Welfare Department to facilitate the setting up of such services.

Photographer: Horace W. Nicholls
Source: IWM Q30034

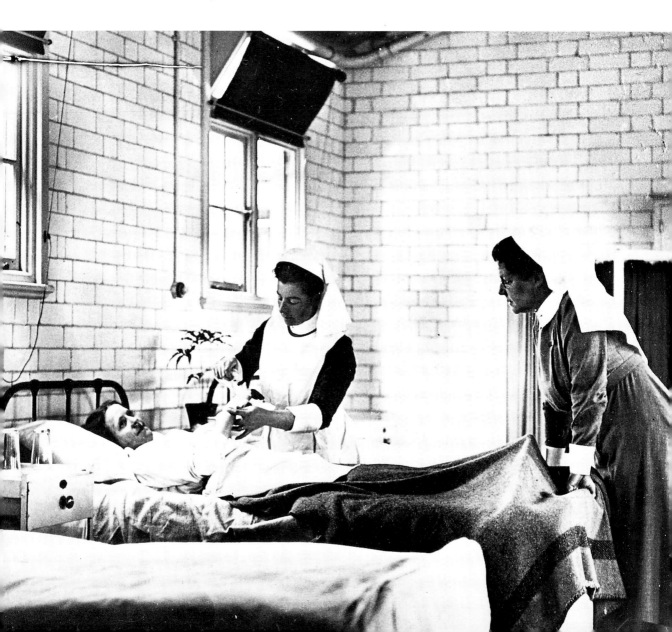

PLATE 60
Queen Mary visiting Woolwich Babies' Home, 5 June 1917

With the influx of women into munitions and other industrial areas the painstaking work of the suffragettes and suffragists for improvement in squalid working and domestic conditions was reinforced by increasing public scrutiny. The Woolwich area of south-east London was dominated by Woolwich Arsenal, which took on huge numbers of women and even introduced a crêche for children. Here Queen Mary visiting the Babies' Home at Woolwich demonstrates the interest in the welfare of women and children she had actively shown from the outbreak of war (see plates 7 and 62). The support of influential women like the Queen helped to convince the public of the importance of such welfare.

Photographer: Unknown
Source: Royal Archives, Queen Mary's Photograph Albums

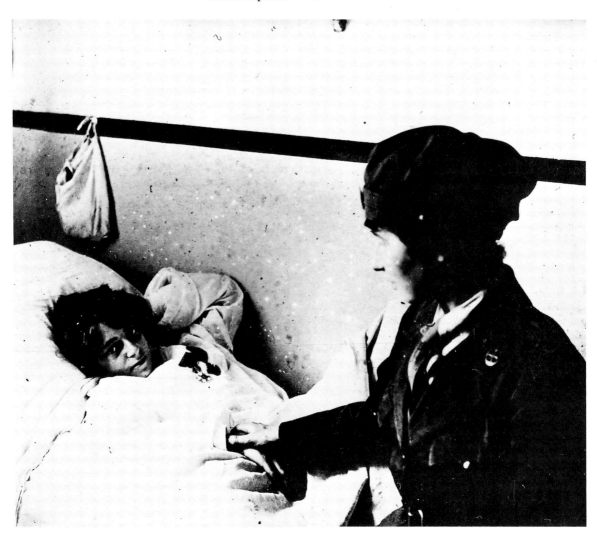

PLATE 61
Henriette Maud Fraser of the FANY, who received the Légion d'Honneur and Croix de Guerre, with Mrs Hamilton Lawrence, who helped to nurse her

Although women's casualties and deaths could not be compared with the massive losses sustained by men, nonetheless the fact that some women had also made the 'supreme sacrifice' did mark a change in public perception. Whether commended for bravery in munitions' explosions or awarded high honours by foreign governments for courage in the battle zones as here, women of all classes could be seen, like Edith Cavell, as 'heroines'. This concept now related women to the public, active, dangerous world hitherto considered unsuitable for them. The women's suffrage groups were not slow to seize this point: by November 1915 the suffrage paper *Votes for Women* was proclaiming 'Votes for Heroines as Well as Heroes'.

Photographer: Unknown
Source: IWM Q107962

PLATE 62
Margaret Bondfield (1873–1953)

Margaret Bondfield was a co-founder with Mary Macarthur of the National Federation of Women Workers. Herself a former shop assistant and daughter of radical working-class parents, she devoted her life to improving the conditions of working women. The war did for her and her colleague Mary Macarthur what their own pioneer efforts could not: it brought them into the centre of power, to serve respectively as member and secretary of the Cabinet's Central Committee for Women's Training and Employment. Mary Macarthur had also secured an unexpected ally in Queen Mary, who worked with both trade union women and set up her own Relief Fund for women. The committee set up training schemes and established a minimum wage of 3d per hour, and a maximum working week of 40 hours. Margaret Bondfield's experience equipped her to become the first woman chairman of the TUC and the first woman Cabinet Minister after the war.

Photographer: Bassano
Source: NPG Ref. neg. no. 59418-1B

PLATE 63
Estelle Sylvia Pankhurst (1882–1960)

Sylvia Pankhurst, daughter of Emmeline Pankhurst and younger sister of Christabel, was with them a founder member of the Women's Social and Political Union, and had shared in the campaigns, imprisonment and forcible feeding of the militant suffragettes before the war. Unlike her mother and sister, she remained committed to the political ideals of the Labour movement and set up her own suffrage group, the East London Federation, when the WSPU moved to the political right. She coped with the immediate hardships of war in the East End by opening cheap restaurants in August 1914, and took on a pub – renamed the 'Mothers' Arms' – to establish a day nursery, clinic and Montessori School. Her League of Rights aimed for better pensions and allowances for working men and women. The final split with her family came on her refusal to support the 'war of iniquity' as she called it; Mrs Pankhurst regretted she could not prevent her using the Pankhurst name. Trained as an art student, Sylvia produced much of the powerful WSPU imagery; her velvet tunic here suggests an artistic rather than political unconventionality.

Photographer: Bassano 1922
Source: NPG Ref. neg. no. 68358-3B

PLATE 64
Women coal workers in a Lancashire colliery, September 1918

The location of this picture is thought to have been the Wigan Coal and Iron Co. Ltd, who, out of a workforce of some 9,000, employed over 500 women on surface work. One-fifth of the male workforce left the coalfields in 1914 to join the Army, and the result was that the industry was left dangerously understaffed. Those men who stayed worked at the coal face, while the surface work was often undertaken by older men, men unfit for military service, young boys and women such as those pictured above. The photographer has left a memorable image of these women in their traditional dress of shawls, clogs and heavy canvas aprons. The picture powerfully conveys their robust pride in their class and their awareness of their own worth. The war was a new experience for women such as these, but they were no strangers to hard work or to anxieties about their menfolk doing a dangerous job.

Photographer: G. P. Lewis
Source: IWM Q28302

CHAPTER IV

FROM FAMILY TO FACTORY

'Without Women Victory Will Tarry'
(Address by David Lloyd George 17 July 1915)

Women's labour extended beyond the traditional domestic role on all fronts, and this was officially accepted and encouraged. The moment when women's private and public role merged was on 17 July 1915 when Mrs Pankhurst led the Women's Right To Serve March through London. The march, financed by the newly formed Ministry of Munitions headed by David Lloyd George, was an admission that the Government now recognised that women's industrial labour was not only useful, but essential. The root cause of this lay in the crisis brought about by the shell shortage; vast areas of heavy industrial production were turned over to munitions of all kinds. Throughout the whole of industry, which was now beginning to adjust to wartime conditions and opportunities, the acute shortage of labour convinced the employers, if not yet the trade unions, that women were essential for skilled as well as unskilled work. In their turn women now came forward in large numbers to take up places on government training schemes. The new and radical approach to the supply of munitions and staffing in the industry was spearheaded by businessmen brought in under the new regime.

It is important to remember that women had always worked in the traditional industries such as coal and textiles, but the labour shortage meant that within these there was now a greater demand and wider opportunities for them. Now in fact women appeared in all industries and public services; they were to be seen working in transport, the public utilities, local authorities, public services, service industries, and vital industries such as food processing. The influx of women into these areas highlighted the appalling industrial conditions. These seemed to have barely improved over the decades, in spite of the efforts of the great Victorian reformers and the existence of the trade unions. Now that women were present in large numbers, conditions hitherto tolerated by men (both employers and employees) were suddenly perceived to be quite unacceptable for women as much for reasons of propriety as for hygiene. Nonetheless standards of cleanliness and comfort still had a long way to go.

Women had won the battle with government and employers; they now had to win over the male trade unions. A compromise was reached which came to be known as 'dilution': male skilled labour could be replaced by female labour for the duration of the war only. Thus the advance of women into trade and industry was seen as a temporary expedient. A further step in state control of industry and the workforce was the introduction of a National Register for all those aged between 15 and 65 years. For the first time women were brought into a direct and personal relationship with the state.

PLATE 65
Woman worker cutting shives in the cooperage of a London brewery, 1918

During the war there was a considerable amount of substitution in breweries on miscellaneous unskilled subsidiary processes: cleaning, bottlewashing, and filling. Women also worked as cellar women, and in the fermentation rooms. Coopering is a skilled trade, and although cutting shives was only a small part of the process, it is probable that this woman had some previous experience of such work. Nicholls took a series of photographs on this occasion which he entitled 'Jolly Brewers'. This photograph has a comfortable rotund quality about it, and the lighting gives the image unexpected delicacy.

Photographer: Horace W. Nicholls
Source: IWM Q31017

PLATE 66
Woman worker using a blow-torch to solder cigarette tins for soldiers, Birmingham, March 1918

The factory in which these tins were made produced jewellery before the war and thus had skilled labour used to intricate work. These particular boxes were made, under contract, for the Princess Mary's Sailors' and Soldiers' Christmas Fund which was inaugurated on 14 October 1914. The Princess issued an appeal for funds from the public in order that a Christmas gift might be sent to all sailors and soldiers at the front on Christmas Day 1914. Such was the response to this appeal that in November it was announced that the scheme would be extended to include all those men and women wearing the King's Uniform on Christmas Day 1914 irrespective of where they were serving. A total of 2,504,677 boxes were made for the Fund. The main supply depot for the brass strip from which the boxes were made was a warehouse in Birmingham, and several of the contractors were located in that city. The main part of the gift consisted of the brass box, containing pipe tobacco and cigarettes for smokers, whilst non-smokers received writing paper. Army nurses, the only women eligible under the terms of the scheme, received a box with 4 oz of chocolate instead of tobacco. There is a nice contrast in the fact that the woman who was engaged in making the boxes worked in fairly primitive conditions without any protection for her eyes, with the consequent hazards, while it was deemed quite improper for women to be officially encouraged to smoke (although smoking by middle- and upper-class women was by no means unknown at this period).

Photographer: Unknown
Source: IWM Q108400

PLATE 67 *Previous page, top left*
Women in the hand finishing shop at the linoleum works of Messrs Barry Ostlers and Shepherd Ltd, Kirkcaldy, Fife, August 1918

Women worked on most of the other processes in the factory, including paint grinding, varnishing and scraping, and on the painting and coating machines as well as the flat printing machines. They worked in the cork mill, stoking the boilers, packing and also in the chemical laboratories. The hand finishing shop seems to have been one of the cleaner areas of the factory, but, although the work was still quite hard, the use of block and tackle for lifting meant that women could cope more easily.

Photographer: G. P. Lewis
Source: IWM Q110054

PLATE 68 *Previous page, bottom left*
Women workers sorting shirts and underclothing at the Dewsbury branch of the Army Ordnance Department, October 1917

Clothes sent back from the Army Depots in France and Flanders, after delousing, were hand sorted by these women. Articles which could be salvaged were repaired, laundered and then re-issued. Clothing unfit to be worn was pulped for fertiliser or turned into rag. This was unskilled, dirty work in unpleasant conditions, but essential if the minimum wastage of precious raw material was to be achieved. There was nothing glamorous about this work and the photographer has starkly conveyed its essential drudgery.

Photographer: Unknown
Source: IWM Q108446

PLATE 69 *Previous page, top right*
Textile worker winding cotton from spools to rollers in a Nottingham lace factory, September 1918

Domestic service aside, the largest pre-war employer of female labour was the textile industry. In 1914 some 863,000 women worked in the factories and mills centred on the traditional textile areas of Lancashire and Yorkshire. Although the overall figure employed in the industry fell towards the end of 1918, women remained a majority in all but the dyeing and bleaching sections where they constituted a mere 20 per cent of the workforce. The lace industry, where demand fell during the war in favour of the more utilitarian and robust fabrics, employed some 20,000 women in 1914 (18,000 men), but by 1918 these figures had dropped by nearly a fifth. In the textile industry as a whole, the overall increase in the numbers of women employed was in the region of 28,000 between 1914 and 1918, in stark contrast to the overall decrease of 68,000 in the number of men.

Photographer: G. P. Lewis
Source: IWM Q28128

PLATE 70 *Previous page, bottom right*
Women chopping and bundling kindling wood, *c.* 1918

This sort of task was commonplace for working-class women, but fuel shortages during the war increased the demand for kindling wood. It is a tribute to the unknown photographer who took this picture that he has managed to endow this very simple and ordinary task with a certain dignity.

Photographer: Unknown
Source: IWM Q109946

PLATE 71 *Previous page, top left*
Women packing flour in the mills of Messrs Rank & Sons, Birkenhead, Lancashire, September 1918

Women undertook most of the heavy work at the mills: landing the sacks of flour from barges, operating grain elevators, maintaining the machinery, 'bran kicking' or filling the sacks of bran, weighing, and sewing the sacks. In the grain-milling industry the great majority of people employed before the war were men and boys, the work of women being almost wholly confined to non-manufacturing processes such as sack repairing. Part of the reason for the lack of women was the relatively heavy nature of the work, and that it was customary to undertake night work, from which women were excluded by virtue of the Factory Acts. This exclusion was waived during the war, and with the introduction of heavy block and tackle and smaller trucks and barrows, it became possible for women's employment to expand. However the trade unions had only agreed to the waiving of the various prohibiting acts for the duration of the war, and it was therefore unlikely that women would retain their foothold in this industry. The majority of women, except in the smaller privately owned family mills, rarely worked the actual milling process, and were mostly found in the warehouses, sacking sheds and cleaning jobs. Some were employed as assistants to the roller men, or in the silo department, and some acted as attendants. They were all required to wear suitable clothing to lessen the risk of accident, as well as for hygiene purposes, but interestingly enough this does not seem to have included any sort of mask, as this photograph shows. Despite the fact that some mill owners expressed the view that women were not suitable to work on milling machinery because of the risk of accidents, no increase in these seems to have resulted from their employment. Approximately 2,000 women were employed in grain-milling in July 1914, and by 1918 this had increased by 9,000, while the number of men so employed had decreased from 40,000 to 32,000 for the same period.

Photographer: G. P. Lewis
Source: IWM Q28268

PLATE 72 *Previous page, bottom left*
Workers at the caustic soda works of Joseph Crossfield & Sons Ltd, Warrington, Lancashire, September 1918

These women are working in dark and grim surroundings on the task of sandwashing silicate of soda used for scrubbing gasses. There was not much propaganda mileage to be gained from this type of image. Indeed the realism of Lewis's work at this juncture owes much to the fact that his brief was to record the work of women in the industrial areas of the Midlands, the north of England and Scotland for the Women's Work Section of the Imperial War Museum.

Photographer: G. P. Lewis
Source: IWM Q109984

PLATE 73 *Previous page, top right*
Women workers for Glasgow Gas Department emptying a coal wagon, 1918

Glasgow Gas Department employed two women to undertake this task starting
in September 1916. Women had been involved in hard manual labour for
centuries, but their rapid spread into the traditional male preserve of heavy
industry concentrated attention on this aspect. For the first time the image of
the working woman is presented officially, in overall and trousers, without
being prettified like the milkmaids and serving maids of popular tradition.

Photographer: Unknown
Source: IWM Q110144

PLATE 74 *Previous page, bottom right*
Labourers employed by Glasgow Gas Department cleaning firebricks, 1918

Women started working on this job in Glasgow in September 1916. Some
fourteen were so employed. Glasgow is a port, and the presence of a black
woman worker, at a period when there was no immigration as such, is a
reminder that there were quite well-established, if small, black communities
in Britain from the nineteenth century, especially in the major ports.

Photographer: Unknown
Source: IWM Q110142

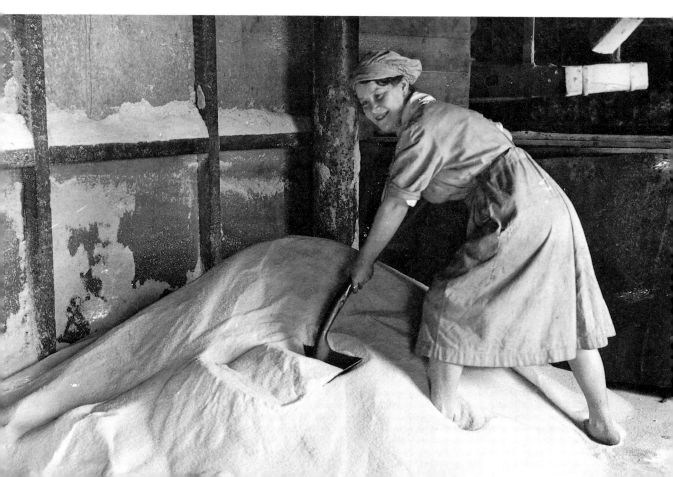

PLATE 75 *Previous page, top left*
Young women workers preparing filter cloths for the sugar presses, Glebe Sugar Refinery, Greenock, Scotland, November 1918

This picture was taken at the same time as Plate 76. The contrast is very marked. Shovelling sugar which had already been refined and was ready for bagging was comparatively clean work. The filter cloth shop, where the cloths were washed, was wet, unpleasant and judging from the faces of these young women, very tiring work. It is difficult to judge the ages of women at this period, but these girls look scarcely out of their teens, and their working conditions, with bare feet on a wet, filthy and, in winter, freezing floor, seem squalid enough to compare with the notorious Victorian industrial environment. This time the photographer has not managed to raise a cheerful smile from his subjects.

Photographer: G. P. Lewis
Source: IWM Q28345

PLATE 76 *Previous page, bottom left*
Woman worker spreading refined sugar before bagging, Glebe Sugar Refinery, Greenock, Scotland, November 1918

Despite the fact that this sugar was presumably going straight from the refinery to the table, the conditions under which it was produced were by no means perfect; still it was, from the workers' point of view, a relatively clean job, certainly one of the better processes in the refining of sugar. The number of women in sugar-refining rose from 11 to 45 per cent of the total personnel: a greater relative increase than in other similar areas such as grain-milling or baking. This was largely a result of greater activity during the war for, though the total amounts of sugar imported into the country fell sharply, the imports of unrefined sugar cane actually increased. Substitution arose therefore as a result of the urgent need for labour, and took place in spite of the fact that most of the work was considered unsuitable for women, given the conditions which then prevailed. Some processes were carried out in great heat, involving heavy lifting and nightwork. Moreover, in some of the older refineries the hygiene facilities were so primitive as to make it unsuitable for men and women to be employed together. The Glebe Sugar Refinery took on 174 women in direct substitution for men.

Photographer: G. P. Lewis
Source: IWM Q28347

PLATE 77 *Previous page, top right*
**Workers stacking barrels at the oil and seed cake works of Messrs Loders &
Mucoline Ltd, Silvertown, London, 1918**

Although the name of Silvertown in East London is probably best known for
the huge TNT explosion which took place in 1917 at Brunner Mond's
Munitions Factory, there were numerous other factories, warehouses and
industries within the dockland complex. Apart from stacking the barrels,
other work carried out by women in this factory included shovelling and
stacking coal for the furnaces, and unloading the empty barrels from the
barges which brought them to the factory wharf. This is a striking image, the
women workers portrayed against the mountain of barrels, with a single male
supervisor. It is also clear that the women had to move the barrels to the top
of the pile without any mechanical aids.

Photographer: Unknown
Source: IWM Q110068

PLATE 78 *Previous page, bottom right*
**Women employees cleaning retort mouthpieces, Glasgow Gas Department,
1918**

Glasgow was in the forefront of the employment of women in the First World
War, initially taking on two women to do this dirty and heavy work in
September 1916. The work of women in Glasgow is one of the best recorded
photographically. The infiltration of women into such varied areas of prime
industrial employment raised conflicting issues, many still unresolved years
later. The justice or otherwise of banning women from certain jobs, and yet
the hardness of the work and conditions prevailing in so many of these, were
just two questions raised; the visual evidence in these photographs still brings
them home with particular vividness.

Photographer: Unknown
Source: IWM Q110150

PLATE 79
**Women porters, Goods Department, South East & Chatham Railway
Company Depot, Bricklayers Arms, Old Kent Road, London, 1918**

These women are moving army stores, which judging by the markings on
the sacks comprise supplies of oats for the Army Service Corps. Much of the
opposition both from employers and male trade unionists to female labour in
industry arose from the received notion that only men were physically able to
carry out the heavier jobs.

Photographer: Unknown
Source: IWM Q110114

PLATE 80
Leather workers at the Pavlova Leather Company's tanning works, Abingdon, Berkshire, 1918

The tanning and currying trade was considered an important field for substitution during the war, owing to the need for huge supplies of leather for the manufacture of military boots, shoes and equipment. Before the war the employment of women was mostly confined to certain of the final currying processes or 'table work' in the manufacture of light leather, and to lighter warehouse work. During the war women were introduced freely into all the final work and also the much more arduous tanning process. The women in this photograph are scraping the hides in order to clean them after the hides have hung in a lime pit to loosen the hair and flesh. This work of 'fleshing' and 'unhairing' was hard and unpleasant. The number of women employed in the trade rose from 9 to 38 per cent, and although a large part of the increase was in the relatively clean and light currying work, in some factories women undertook virtually all the processes – but under male supervision.

Photographer: Unknown
Source: IWM Q110014

PLATE 81
London General Omnibus Company bus conductress in summer uniform, 1918

The bus is a 'B' Type, similar to those which were sent to France to transport men up to the front. The progress of women in this section of the transport services was relatively slow but marked, although in real terms it was shortlived, and did not really become established until the Second World War. By far the largest proportion of women, in spite of the example of the Glasgow Tramways Department (see Plate 91), were employed on the buses as conductresses. Male opposition to the advent of women was considerable. The Amalgamated Association of Tramway and Vehicle Workers had opened their membership to women, but prejudice was implicit in the Tramway Workers' resolution of May 1915, which emphasised that the employment of women in such work was 'dangerous' and 'unwise'. In fact it was not until February 1916 that the London General Omnibus Company started to employ women. Only 100 had started work by March, although the training schemes were designed to provide an increase of 500 a month. By the following year the figure had risen to around 2,500, many of whom were former domestic servants escaping drudgery and at the same time doing 'their bit' both for their country, and perhaps for their former employers, who now found it 'unpatriotic' to have more than the minimum number of servants.

Photographer: Unknown
Source: IWM Q109768

PLATE 82
Women ticket collectors at the Great Western Railway Terminus at Paddington, 10 April 1915

At the outbreak of war women fulfilled a number of functions on the railways such as booking clerks, telegraph and telephone operators, carriage cleaners and charwomen; they also worked on the clerical side and in domestic service in the railway companies' hotels and restaurants. There were 12,423 women thus employed. Four years later this figure had risen to over 65,000 and included those doing what might be termed 'new' jobs like the two women in this photograph, who must have been amongst the earliest. The impact of women in the transport industries particularly on the railways was short-lived, and the 'high profile' nature of work such as ticket collecting did not really reflect where the main increase in women's labour lay. It was in the clerical and telephone side of the industry that the rate of increase was most noticeable. That figure rose from 2,800 in 1914 to just short of 21,000 by 1918. It was in fact in general office work where women were to gain a lasting foothold.

Photographer: Unknown
Source: IWM Q28025

PLATE 83
Postwomen outside a district sorting office

61,000 women were employed in the Post Office, mainly in clerical and cleaning jobs before the First World War, and about 189,000 men, on postal deliveries, sorting, and telephones. By 1918 the latter figure had dropped by 80,000 while the number of women employed had increased by some 60,000. The latter rise, while considerable in itself, is of more significance in that with the increase in numbers came the increase in the variety of work women could undertake. By 1920 54,000 of these women were no longer employed, and indeed the male workforce had declined to 67,000 compared with the pre-war figure. The date of this photograph is uncertain, but the absence of uniforms for the women would suggest that it is quite early. The variety of hats here were soon replaced by smart broad-brimmed navy blue straw, and the women wore white shirts, navy blue ties, navy blue jackets and skirts trimmed with red.

Photographer: Unknown
Source: IWM Q61349

PLATE 84
Woman parcel truck driver, Great Eastern Railway Company, 1918

This cheerful young woman driving a battery-powered Railodok parcel truck for the Great Eastern Railway Company has improved on the standard issue uniform by a very fashionable pair of stockings and smart, but definitely non-regulation shoes. Again it is interesting to see how once uniform is achieved as the desirable emblem of status, and becomes commonplace, there emerges an impulse to individualise it.

Photographer: Unknown
Source: IWM Q27983

PLATE 85
Woman guard on a London Underground train, 1918

Women working in public transport were the highly visible side of the progress which women had made in employment. The travelling public saw these women constantly and perhaps judged their effectiveness and those of women in general as a result. Most ordinary people, whilst aware of the increase in the employment of women, had little or no direct contact with them and the extent and diversity of women's war work was probably not fully realised until after hostilities had ceased.

Photographer: Unknown
Source: IWM Q110106

PLATE 86

Window cleaners for the Mayfair Window Cleaning Company setting out on their rounds, 1918

The impression that is often conveyed by any survey of women's work in the First World War is that it was wholly directed towards the prosecution of the war, in that much is made of the women who went into munitions and other similar 'front line' jobs. In fact, life had to continue as usual, roads had to be swept and, as in this case labour had to be found to clean windows. This was where the true nature of what came to be called 'substitution' is most simply illustrated. Women substituted in the window-cleaning business for the men who had left the work to enter the Services. When the war ended the men came back, and the women, for the most part, reverted to their former, more domestic occupations. On a pleasant warm summer day it is possible to imagine that cleaning windows could be a reasonably enjoyable pastime. On what was clearly a wet day, and in the cold weather it must have been a hard way to earn a living.

Photographer: Unknown
Source: IWM Q109770

PLATE 87
A shipyard worker and her horse at the Govan Shipyard of Harland and Wolff Ltd on the Clyde, 28 June 1918

Unfortunately the name of the horse is not recorded, but its handler was a shipyard worker at Govan Shipyard called Susie Loftus. Her job was to take charge of the horse which hauled the plates for the shell platers to the various ships under construction in the yards. It must be said, however, that as it is unlikely that the horse made trips at this pace day in and day out, it is tempting to speculate whether the photographer might not have suggested that on this occasion they should take the ramp 'at the run'. Nonetheless it is a wonderful photograph, full of life and action.

Photographer: Unknown
Source: IWM Q110081

PLATE 89 *Opposite, top*
Women workers at Messrs Thew, Hooker Silby Ltd, Buckinghamshire, 1918

Women did almost all the jobs which made up milk processing. These included collecting the churns, weighing, condensing, drying and packaging as well as making the packing crates for the finished product and driving the lorries. Fresh milk supplies were at a premium, particularly for the troops at the front. One of the products produced by women such as these was the almost universal milk substitute, tinned condensed milk, a thick, white and very sweet mixture fondly remembered by many. Tea, by now the universal British panacea, suffered from the addition of condensed milk (although it benefited from a dash of rum). Cocoa and chocolate, however, both of which were widely consumed at this period, were in the view of many greatly improved with a spoonful of condensed milk.

Photographer: G. P. Lewis
Source: IWM Q110055

PLATE 90 *Opposite, below*
Carters employed by the South East & Chatham Railway leaving their depot at the Bricklayers Arms, Old Kent Road, London, 1918

Women drove horse-drawn carts and small wagons in the country districts but until the war few had done so in London; even fewer would have had experience of driving wagons of this size and weight. The railway companies were the chief employers of female labour in this sphere of substitution, although some of the removal and delivery firms also took on women as drivers. They were provided with thick overcoats, stout shoes with gaiters, and in some instances with rough serge 'bloomers' which were probably easier and more appropriate wear when getting on and off the driving seat.

Photographer: Unknown
Source: IWM Q110112

PLATE 91
Corporation of Glasgow Tramways Department, Electrical Sub-Station Attendant, 1918

Because Glasgow Tramways Department was the first to employ women actually on the vehicles, it is easy to overlook the extent to which women were employed behind the scenes. Glasgow Tramways started to employ women as Sub-Station Attendants in May 1916, when ten were taken on. On average they earned 35/6d, including bonus, for a 42-hour week. Working conditions here were generally good, and attracted women from the better-educated classes. Here women were offered measurable responsibility despite the initial and, in some cases, lasting objections of men, who regarded this as skilled work, and therefore the preserve of male workers alone. This woman wears no uniform and can be smartly dressed for her work.

Photographer: Unknown
Source: IWM Q110153

PLATE 92
**Assistant in charge of the Receiving Room, Glasgow Corporation Weights
and Measures Department, 11 October 1918**

This woman was the only one carrying out this task, although other women
worked in different areas of the department. She started work in 1915 at
33/- a week, including bonuses, for a 44-hour week. These images of female
clerks and office workers are less arresting than those of women in heavy
industry, but they represent a more permanent change in work available to
women.

Photographer: Unknown
Source: IWM Q110170

PLATE 93

A woman fitter at work on the rear axle of a bus in the London General Omnibus Company's workshops, 1918

This type of work was virtually unknown to women before the First World War, and yet they carried out the overhaul and general servicing of vehicles throughout the war as though they had been doing the work most of their lives. Few would have been able to put their mechanical knowledge to good use at the end of the war, since the employment of women in this area of engineering was acceptable to the unions for the duration of hostilities only. This simple but telling image is a rare example of a woman not apparently posing for the shot but seeming absorbed in her task.

Photographer: Unknown
Source: IWM Q110109

PLATE 94 *Opposite*

Worker operating a machine for centering studded tread on motor tyres: Charles Mackintosh and Sons Ltd, rubber factory, Manchester, September 1918

The rubber industry employed large numbers of women. At one factory in Birmingham 80 per cent of the workforce were women, the only male labour being used on heavy machinery. Apart from tyres these factories produced gloves, hot water bottles, rubber cushions, and gas mask tubes. Mackintosh and Sons also gave their name to the rubber weatherproof coat, or 'mackintosh' although, as many of the photographs of women working outdoors show, its use was not yet widespread.

Photographer: G. P. Lewis
Source: IWM Q28235

PLATE 95 *Previous page, top left*
Women retort house workers, South Metropolitan Gas Co, Old Kent Road, London, June 1918

The gas companies employed large numbers of women on several different tasks, and a great deal of their time seems to have been taken up with loading and delivering coke. These women, working in the retort house, show another side of women's labour in this industry, which supplied much of the power for heating, and much of the lighting for streets, shops and private housing. Skirts would have been quite out of place in this type of work which was hot, dirty and potentially hazardous. Lewis has managed to portray these women with reticence, but the flames shooting up in front of the open retorts provide a dramatic illustration of the power generated and controlled by the women.

Photographer: G. P. Lewis
Source: IWM Q109989

PLATE 96 *Previous page, bottom left*
Women carpenters employed by Tarrants to construct huts for the British troops serving in France, 1918

Carpentry, was a skilled trade, traditionally reserved for men, in which women proved themselves proficient. It is the sight of women in jobs such as these (here wearing a non-uniform collection of overalls), rather than the familiar VADs, which brings home the potentially radical change in notions of the role of women at this time.

Photographer: Unknown
Source: IWM Q6765

PLATE 97 *Previous page, top right*
Shipyard workers, Palmers Shipbuilding Yard, Hebburn-on-Tyne, *c.* 1918

These girls were employed solely in lifting and carrying timber round the yard, but in other areas of the shipbuilding industry women did every possible sort of job: riveting, welding, labouring and painting. The ship tied up to the quay is painted in 'Dazzle' – a technique invented in the First World War for camouflage at sea.

Photographer: G. P. Lewis
Source: IWM Q110071

PLATE 98 *Opposite page, bottom right*
Women workers sewing asbestos mattresses used for lining boilers in battleships, Messrs Turner Brothers Abestos Factory, Trafford Park, Manchester, September 1918

Asbestos was not then recognised as the health hazard which it is today. However, many of those who worked in close proximity to the material used to suffer from what they called 'asbestos throat', and one worker (not one of

Turner's), recorded that she and her colleagues were often knee deep in the stuff. The protection of workers from dangerous industrial processes still had a long way to go, and it was the introduction of women into the industrial labour force which increased awareness of the need for safer conditions.

Photographer: G. P. Lewis
Source: IWM Q28240

PLATE 99 *Over, top left*
Men and women workers filling shells at the Chilwell Factory, Nottingham, 1918

Chilwell was one of the largest munitions factories and comprised a huge complex of buildings in which any number of different processes were carried out. Judging from this picture the shells seem to have been loaded into small wagons and rolled under the taps to be filled from the large tank overhead. Men and women workers wore much the same type of protective clothing and those doing the actual filling wore protective face masks. Chilwell was later often referred to as the 'VC' factory in recognition of the gallantry of its staff during an explosion in one of the sheds, which resulted in a large number of fatal casualties.

Photographer: Horace W. Nicholls
Source: IWM Q30028

PLATE 100 *Over, bottom left*
Miss Lilian Barker, OBE, with women workers in the TNT Department, Quick Firing Cartridge Factory No 4, Woolwich Arsenal, May 1918

Women working on processes which involved putting TNT into the shells suffered a very visible health hazard: their faces and hands turned yellow. These women who suffered from TNT poisoning were nicknamed 'canaries'. Although women were carefully checked to make sure their standard of health was up to the work, most only lasted a matter of a fortnight or three weeks at a time in the TNT shops before having to move to other jobs in the factory. The welfare of munitions girls was of prime importance and the Welfare Section of the Ministry of Munitions was very active in its concern for the girls' physical health and their social wellbeing. Lilian Barker, who became a legend, had been in the forefront of women's involvement from the early days of the war. She had been Principal of the London County Council Women's Institute in Conway Street, Marylebone, and later set up the cookery section of the Women's Legion, before moving to Woolwich to supervise the women workers. Later she went on to become Governor of the Women's Prison at Aylesbury. The extent to which women became the major force in munitions work can be illustrated by comparison with Woolwich's pre-war employment of women. Before 1914 only 10 women were employed in the Royal Factories, and these at the Ordnance Factory at Woolwich. Four years later these 10 had been joined by an additional 24,030. At Enfield, none had been employed before the war; by the end of the war the figure was 1,500. These increases were reflected throughout the munitions industry.

Photographer: Unknown
Source: IWM Q27889

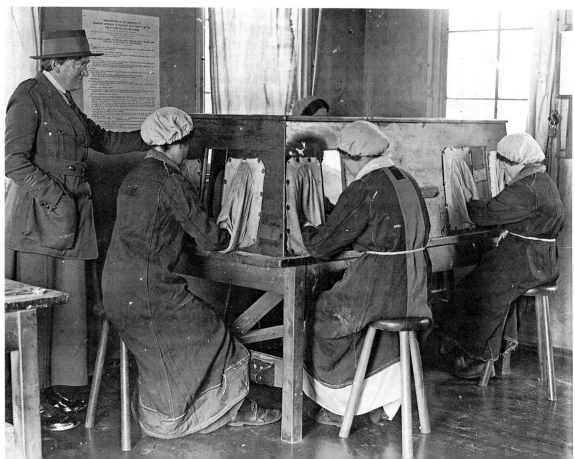

PLATE 101
A woman worker acetylene welding the body of an aerial bomb, 1918

The Ministry of Munitions instituted training schemes often held at local schools or Technical Colleges to teach women the basic skills of work such as welding, at which many became very proficient. Though this woman is wearing protective goggles and a leather apron, she looks in less danger from the welding equipment than from having her feet crushed by the bomb. The whole set-up looks unstable, the bomb being supported at one end by what is obviously a wooden stool, and at the other by a contraption of wooden box, a small shell set at right angles and what looks like a mortar baseplace.

Photographer: Unknown
Source: IWM Q54631

PLATE 102
Woman worker fitting sections to the templates of aeroplane propellers, Frederick Tibbenham Ltd, Turret Lane, Ipswich, Suffolk, c. 1918

'Munitions' did not only mean the manufacture of shells and bombs. In the production of aeroplanes at this period, the skills of the woodworker and joiner were very much to the fore, and before the war few women had any skills in this trade. The manufacture of aircraft parts was a highly skilled precision-based business, and young girls and women were found to be particularly adept at learning the trade. It is as well to remember that their skills tended to be confined to a particular process and, because they had not completed the necessary years of apprenticeship required by boys entering the joinery trade, their ability to find a career in the woodworking industry after the war was severely limited.

Photographer: Unknown
Source: IWM Q109783

PLATE 103
Women workers at Vickers Ltd, May 1917

These women are working lathes, turning brass nose cones for shells. This was precision machine work and, although the lathes would have been set up by skilled male labour, such work in an established firm such as Vickers marked yet another point in the progress of women in industry. This photograph illustrates the intensive nature of the job in a huge workshop where the noise must have been considerable. There are no signs of any safety guards at the lathes, although workers were issued with protective clothing and had to keep their hair short, or covered, to prevent accidents.

Photographer: Unknown
Source: IWM Q108473

PLATE 104
Operator hand stemming a 9.2 inch high explosive artillery shell after filling with Amatol, National Shell Filling Factory No. 14, Hereford, 1917

The National Shell Filling Factories, which were dotted all over the country, absorbed far and away the largest number of women employed in munitions and its associated work. No women had been employed at the outbreak of war, but by 1916 there were 18,460; by 1917 when figures were at their peak 55,440, and in 1918 53,290. The NSFF were often temporary wooden structures, cold, draughty and, no doubt to the relief of the local inhabitants, usually situated miles from any centre of population. Travelling times and distances were considerable, and the normal shift of 10 to 12 hours often extended to over 15 by the time the worker had got to and from work. There were hostels, but again these were usually some distance away. In relative terms the munitions workers were well paid, and for that reason often the subject of some envy from other workers who were paid less and whose contribution was less widely publicised. Even in training the pay was 15/– to 25/–, and when qualified the women could earn bonuses above the basic rates, sometimes amounting to as much as £2.10s a week. Women in the munitions industry were known as 'Munitionettes' – an interesting example, like 'suffragette', of the impulse to classify women with a nickname once they became publicly visible as a group.

Photographer: Unknown
Source: IWM Q70679

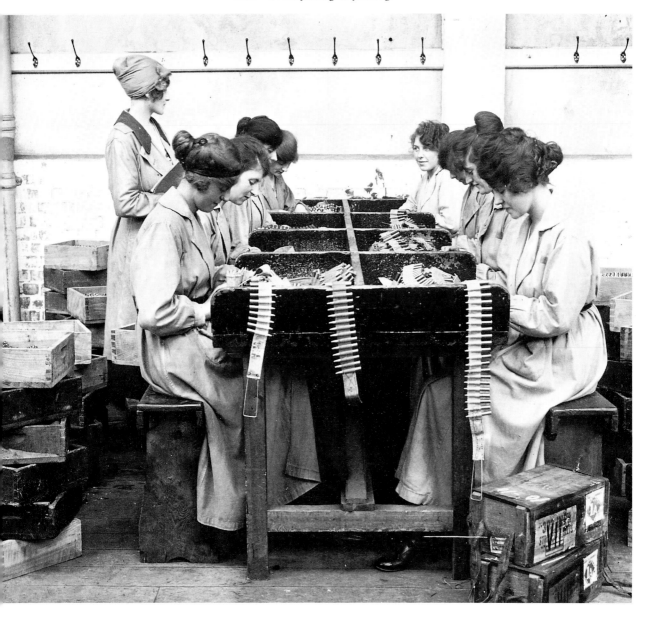

PLATE 105
**Munitions workers filling machine gun ammunition belts in the Inspection
Buildings at the Park Royal Factory, north-west London,** *c.* **1918**

This photograph contrasts interestingly with plate 100 taken at Woolwich.
Here the process is relatively clean; the girls are neatly dressed and quite
clearly well aware that their photograph is being taken. The lady supervisor
is an interesting contrast to the rather masculine image of Miss Barker.

Photographer: Horace W. Nicholls
Source: IWM Q31314

PLATE 106

Funeral procession of a munitions worker killed on duty, Swansea, August Bank Holiday Monday, 1917

The funeral was held on the Bank Holiday. This is a curious, and rather touching mixture of the civilian and the military funeral. The coffin is covered in the Union Flag (a privilege normally only extended to servicemen and women or retired members of HM Forces) and escorted by eight pall bearers dressed in munitions workers' uniforms; the girl nearest the camera is wearing the brass triangular 'On War Service' badge issued to all women who worked in munitions factories. They clearly considered that this woman had died in the service of her country and was as much a casualty of the war as the soldier dying at the front. The making of munitions was a hazardous business, but deaths were comparatively rare. What made the death of any woman in such circumstances a matter for comment was that hitherto they had not been in situations where it could happen. The public character of such funerals brought home to many people the nature of women's involvement in the war.

Photographer: Unknown
Source: IWM Q108454

CHAPTER V

SERVANTS OF THE STATE

'The Girl Behind the Man Behind the Gun'
(Caption from a recruiting poster)

For women, uniform had become the desirable symbol of allegiance to an ideal cause. It had been adopted by the private organisations, although in almost all cases it represented the voluntary commitment of one individual to another or, as with nurses, a public acknowledgement of a private duty. The uniforms worn by women from 1917, when the first of the Women's Services was formed, still contained these elements, but in addition came the public recognition of a personal duty which as citizens they owed to the state. For the first time women wore official uniform in the service of their country.

The wearing of uniform by women once again brought out the ambivalence of the public attitude: the Army, while publicly celebrated, was privately shunned; the only acceptable face being that of the 'officer and gentleman'. It was this glamorous tradition that middle- and upper-class women wished to embrace. The problem elsewhere was twofold. First was the ingrained British suspicion of a standing army based at home potentially available for use by the civil power. Second was the old reputation of the 'other ranks' for licentiousness and drunken behaviour. This last was rooted in the perennial problem of class relations – the upper classes in civilian life in fact felt threatened by what they perceived to be the ignorance and unruliness of the working classes.

The enthusiasm of middle- and upper-class women for military-style uniforms resulted from their own class assumptions about the social composition of the Armed Forces. To them the 'real' Army and Navy were the 'officers and gentlemen' whose ethos they wished to share in their own organisations. The problematic consequences of this became clear once the need for official Women's Services emerged. These required many more women to undertake the tasks of 'other ranks' than had the private organisations. As Lady Londonderry had found with the Women's Legion, lower-middle- and working-class women were much more suspicious of the Forces. They disapproved of the ordinary servicemen whom they regarded as morally reprobate and avoided them. This attitude only changed when the composition of the army itself changed, with the influx of thousands of 'respectable' men who answered Lord Kitchener's call in 1914. The notion of women in uniform and in the public eye had also become more generally acceptable. Finally the official Women's Services offered what the private organisations had not: a reasonable rate of pay, though it was not comparable to that of the men. Despite women's very real desire to express their patriotism in this way, neither the military authorities nor society as a whole would accept the implications of integrating the Women's Services into the Armed Forces. Their legal status remained that of civilians, and one advantage of this was that it enabled the leaders of the women's organisations who took over to keep the control of conditions of service out of the hands of the military.

On the Home Front the concept of a uniformed and disciplined service extended to those women officially recruited to work on the land. For centuries women had worked on the land, but by 1914 the number in permanent full-time employment had drastically fallen. There were several reasons for this, the most notable being a general decline in agriculture owing to cheap imports from the Empire, and the increasing mechanisation of the work. The consequent low agricultural wage levels led to an exodus from the countryside into the thriving centres of industry. The fortunes of agriculture were reversed as the importance of home-grown foodstuffs was emphasised by the war which curtailed the import of foreign produce.

Experience proved that voluntary and seasonal work fragmented the effort to make the land more productive. This state of affairs was heightened by the increasing shortage of male labour as established workers left to join the Army. Yet again the state had to intervene. It set up regional agricultural committees with responsibility for the land and the organisation and direction of labour, which included the various women's agricultural groups.

PLATE 107 *See page 114*
Members of the Women's Army Auxiliary Corps employed in the Army bakery, Dieppe, 10 February 1918

The WAAC owed its origins to a decision taken in January 1917 to employ women in the Lines of Communication in France. The announcement of the formation of the Corps appeared in the press on 20 February, and the official instrument by which the Corps was brought into existence was the Army Council Instruction published on 28 March. Three days later on 31 March 1917 the first draft of women for employment with the Army in France left London, travelling to Boulogne from Folkestone. In the first instance the women were to be employed in the Expeditionary Force Canteens to replace men needed in the front line. But it was not long before they occupied posts as clerks, cooks, telephonists, storekeepers, worked on the Army printing presses, and for the Ordnance Survey (the Southampton civil servants enrolled *en masse* when the section was transferred to France). An army is supposed to march on its stomach; it certainly fights more effectively if it is well fed, and this photograph of four pleasant, cheerful young women loading bread on to shelves must have been reassuring in more ways than one. The WAACs were the subject of endless gossip concerning their behaviour in France, but like much of that sort of talk it was found to have no real substance.

The image of women engaged upon what were really only extensions or larger-scale additions of their normal domestic work at home offered some reassurance as to conditions both for women and for men. The objection to women being granted Commissioned rank which had arisen in the medical services still remained: the head of the WAAC, Mrs Chalmers Watson, was known as Chief Controller and, like her fellow 'officers', did not receive the King's Commission.

Photographer: Unknown
Source: IWM Q8477

PLATE 108
Ratings of the Women's Royal Naval Service serving in the canteen at the Royal Marine Barracks, Chatham, Kent, summer 1918

Despite its understandable claims to be the 'senior service', the Women's Royal Naval Service was not formed until November 1917, and thus had, as events were to prove, a very short existence within the scope of this book. It has never been a large Service even in war, and right from the beginning always prided itself on its special place. The uniform was adapted from the traditional form, complete with sailor collars, smart and unfussy; unlike its sister Services, the WRNS did not go in for any more than the basic adornments deemed necessary to indicate rank or job. These two women in their rough serge navy blue uniform dresses wear on their right sleeves the blue embroidered 'category' badge of crossed keys, which proclaimed their trade: porters, messengers or, as in this case, storekeepers. Chatham, or 'Chats' in naval slang, was one of the largest of the naval bases and, because it was a permanent base, already had a well-established infrastructure of married and single accommodation. The canteen at the Royal Marine Barracks served the needs of the Marines' families as well as the men. The men are Royal Marine Artillery and the unfamiliar headdress, called a 'Brodrick', was worn by the RMA from 1902 to 1921.

Photographer: G. P. Lewis
Source: IWM Q19770

PLATE 109

WRNS Ratings, based at Lowestoft on the Suffolk coast, painting mines and steel floats, summer 1918

Lewis took this photograph on the quayside at Lowestoft as one of a series depicting the WRNS on the east coast of England. Lowestoft, an ancient fishing port, was an important base for minesweepers and small craft. Not only was it strategically placed opposite the North Sea German naval ports, but it was also important because of the wealth of seafaring knowledge which the navy used to good effect, since most small craft – such as minesweepers – were manned by trawlermen serving in the RNVR. These WRNS, in their immaculate caps with white summer tops and cap or tally ribbons, were more than likely local women, known in the Women's Services as 'Immobiles'. 'Mobiles' could be posted anywhere in the country; 'Immobiles' were enrolled to serve at home in their own towns, or nearby, and many lived at home rather than in quarters. The WRNS followed the example of the wartime Royal Navy in not wearing a ship's name on their tally ribbon but, whereas the men merely had the letters 'HMS', the women had 'WRNS' with a gold fouled anchor in the centre. The irony was that these two WRNS were about as close to the sea as they would ever be during their service. The WRNS took as their unofficial motto 'Never at Sea', since long tradition meant that they could not serve aboard ship.

Photographer: G. P. Lewis
Source: IWM Q19649

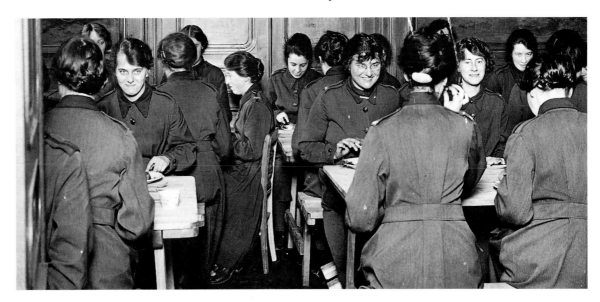

PLATE 110
Members of the Women's Army Auxiliary Corps in their mess room, Rouen, 24 July 1917

These women were among those employed in the Record Office with the 3rd Echelon at Rouen. The WAACs were under the control of Area Controllers: the first for the Rouen Area was Miss F. Wade, who took up her appointment on 1 July 1917, but owing to sickness was relieved later by Miss Lila Davy, who became one of the most influential figures in the new corps. Accommodation for the women in France had been a matter of concern from the outset. The Army recognised that not only was normal basic accommodation as offered to the men unsuitable for women, but if the men saw women living in less than suitable conditions it might also well prove bad for morale. In fact, the women would have put up with a lot less, and there was some resentment amongst the men that it cost more to house the women. In general the women were given quarters in permanent buildings where possible, and it was only later, after the enemy air raids on some of the camps, that the women had to resort to tented shelter for their own safety. The furniture in this rather opulent mess room is basic army trestle tables and benches or rough chairs. The girls' hair, almost always worn long at this period, is put up neatly, and the not very flattering dresses (which were a curious grey brown rather than khaki) look neat and utilitarian. The shoulder straps bore the title 'WAAC', rather in the same way the men wore the title of their regiment or corps; the central strip on the shoulder strap carried different colours for the various branches: clerical, cookery, motor section and so on. The women's messes were, like the men's, segregated; that is the officers, (or Administrators as the women were called) messed separately from the rank and file, who were called Workers in the case of the 'Privates', and Forewomen in that of the 'NCOs'.

Photographer: Unknown
Source: IWM Q5756

PLATE 111
Women's Army Auxiliary Corps Cooks tending fat boilers in an infantry camp, Rouen, 24 July 1917

Women were sent to France in the first place to relieve men on the Lines of Communication by doing work such as cooking. Unglamorous though it was, this remained their main function and soon extended beyond cooking for officers, in their clubs behind the lines, to preparing meals for the men nearer the front. The type of stove was called a Soyer Stove. Again it is the appearance of women undertaking these tasks that focuses the eye on the primitive resources and the dusty surroundings where they worked.

Photographer: Unknown
Source: IWM Q5740

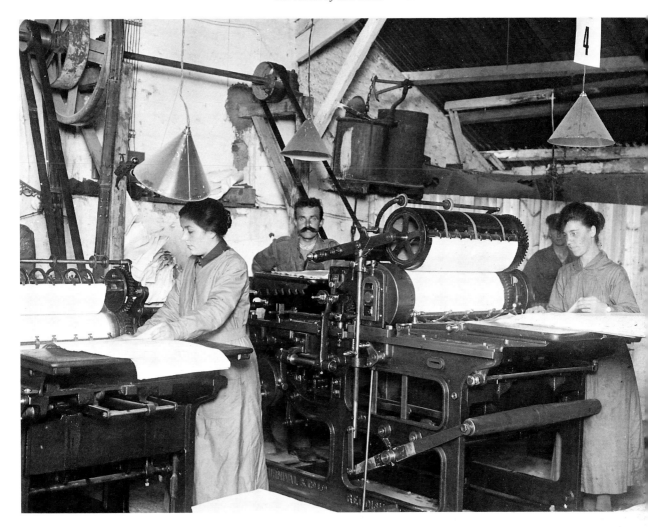

PLATE 112
**WAACs tending presses in the Army Printing Works, Abbéville, France,
19 September 1917**

Women had little or no opportunity to operate printing presses in civilian
life: indeed the printing trades were almost exclusively male dominated. But
the Army, unhampered by the restrictive practices of the civilian trades,
needed to release able-bodied men from work that could just as well be done
by women. The army organisation in France produced millions of records,
many of which had to be printed and circulated on the spot. This photograph
would suggest that the men stood by while the women did the work, but
that is unlikely to have been the case. Printing, or working the presses, was
a new job for women and the propaganda value of such a picture would be
immense when seen by those at home in Britain. The presses were set up in
a permanent building requisitioned by the Army for the purpose.

Photographer: Unknown
Source: IWM Q5963

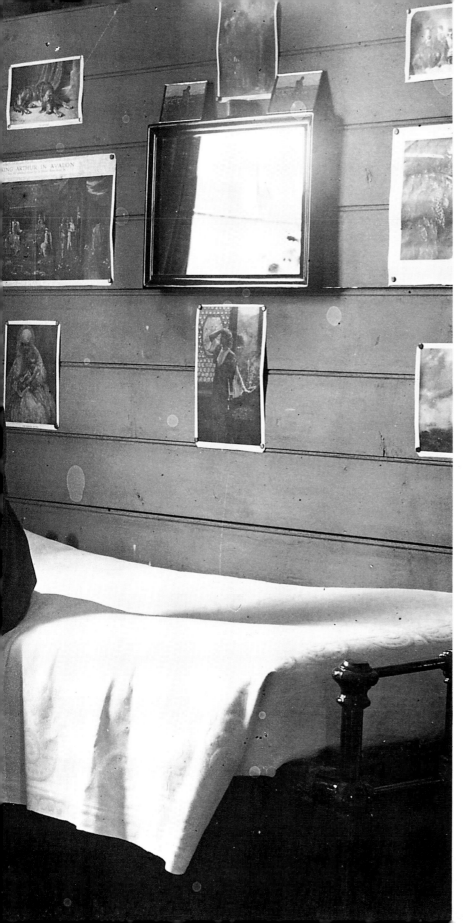

PLATE 113
Women's Royal Naval Service Ratings in their quarters at Osea Island, in the Blackwater Estuary, Essex, summer 1918

The WRNS at Osea Island, which was a coastal motor-boat base during the First World War, lived in wooden huts, two to a cubicle. The accommodation varied enormously in each establishment, but it was always very basic, and the women themselves made their living areas as comfortable as possible, with flowers, china ornaments, photographs, and pictures from books and periodicals. The Wren on the right has displayed an interesting mixture of prints: religious scenes, dogs and tales from the Arthurian legends. The bedspreads were standard Royal Navy issue, as were the iron bedsteads and wooden chests of drawers. This is one of a series of photographs which G. P. Lewis took on his travels between July and November 1918, and has a still and reflective quality. Privacy was precious to any serviceman or servicewoman, in a system which required a great deal of conformity, and the ability to stamp a little of their own personality on their surroundings was vitally important. In other bases, the women lived in barracks, or, as some did in Portsmouth, in Millar's Hotel. The officers on Osea Island had better accommodation in one of the houses.

Photographer: G. P. Lewis
Source: IWM Q19749

PLATE 114

Locator Card Section, Queen Mary's Army Auxiliary Corps with the American Expeditionary Force at Bourges. On the left, standing, is the QMAAC Technical Administrator Miss Bigge, and on the right, seated and wearing the hat, is Miss Starr, a Red Cross Worker, March 1919

This is one of the series of photographs taken by Olive Edis. At the beginning of June 1918, it was decided that the WAACS (QMAAC was never, it seems, used in conversation) should be attached to the American Expeditionary Force which, to save shipping space, had come to Europe with the minimum of administrative personnel. The women attached to the AEF were to be independent from the British armies in France and had their own Chief Controller. On 11 July the first draft of women went from Harve to Tours where General Pershing's Headquarters had been set up. Conditions at Tours were far from satisfactory, although they improved after 23 September when the majority accompanied the American Record Office to Bourges where the camp in which they lived was well set up and comfortable. The employment of the QMAACs with the AEF was a conspicuous success, and the women were highly thought of by the American authorities. It is difficult to realise now what a remarkable association this was: very few British women, other than those from the upper classes who had travelled in North America, would ever have met an American before, or have heard one speak. Few Americans also would ever have left their own towns, let alone travelled overseas and met women from respectable backgrounds who spoke their own language. There is no evidence that this first forging of Anglo-American relations led to any significant or lasting associations (no GI brides in that war), but the Americans, with their informality and habitual courtesy to women, must have made a refreshing change from the sometimes stuffy and stiffly correct attitude of the British officers.

Photographer: Olive Edis
Source: IWM Q8056

PLATE 115
WRNS Officer instructing Ratings in the use of Anti-Gas Respirators, Lowestoft, summer 1918

The contrasting uniforms of the categories of WRNS is well illustrated in this photograph. The WRNS Officer, an Assistant Principal, wore a tailored uniform jacket which, apart from the way it buttoned, was virtually identical to that worn by Royal Navy Officers. It had eight gilt buttons, and the rank lace was blue, not gold. Originally there were two classes of officers: Directors, who wore the diamond above the stripe, and Principals who did not. Later the distinction was abolished and all officers wore the diamond, which was the WRNS equivalent of the so called 'executive curl' which RN Officers wore above their rank lace. The WRNS rating being instructed in the use of the Naval Box Respirator – a Petty Officer – wore a rough serge jacket and skirt with white shirt and collar and black tie. There is no record of Servicewomen coming into contact with poison gas, although in Belgium Mairi Chisholm and Elsie Knocker were both gassed (see Plate 33).

Photographer: G. P. Lewis
Source: IWM Q19655

PLATE 116 *Previous page, left*
Members of the Queen Mary's Army Auxiliary Corps (formerly WAAC) working in the stores office at the 61st Advanced Motor Transport Section at Abbéville. In charge of the section is the Technical Administrator, Miss Nicholls, standing on the left facing the camera, March 1919

This is one of a series of photographs taken by Olive Edis during her month-long tour of France and Belgium in March 1919. Miss Edis was invited to undertake the work of recording women's contribution to the war effort on the Western Front by Miss Agnes Conway and Lady Priscilla Norman, of the Women's Work Section of the Imperial War Museum. Olive Edis's pictures are therefore very much a woman's view of other women, recorded at the behest of a committee of women which believed it vital to record the work for posterity. The committee was also convinced that women would not need to carry out similar work in the future, and would be returning to a society which would either forget, or not even have known, that they had ever made such a contribution. Despite the obviously military nature of the work and the surroundings, it is difficult to suppress the image of the classroom, with the teacher and the prefects. Interestingly enough this flavour seemed to permeate all Miss Edis's work on this particular assignment.

Photographer: Olive Edis
Source: IWM Q8048

PLATE 117 *Previous page, right*
Queen Mary's Army Auxiliary Corps Camp No. 4, Rouen, a general view of the Nissen huts, March 1919

Despite several attempts to start for France before the end of hostilities in November 1918, Olive Edis, escorted by Lady Norman and Agnes Conway did not begin recording the work of women in France until March 1919. To some extent this late beginning meant that the images she recorded lacked the immediate impact of the earlier ones; on the other hand, in the aftermath of war there was time for reflection and for a more considered approach. Whilst the earlier pictures had a real propaganda value which incidentally became a record for posterity, Edis's photographs were almost wholly shot with a view to recording the places and people for the future. Thus their importance lies in a different sphere. They well illustrate the wartime conditions in which the women who went to France lived, as well as presenting the calm after the storm. The war was over, and for the women at No. 4 Camp at Rouen the future was made up of measurable time. Their lives were less frenetic, the danger had gone, and the hours off duty were spent making a fairly dull and rather forbidding environment more pleasant. The camp is very basic, but neat and contained, with electric light in the huts. It is tempting to see the rows of huts either side of the central pavement area as being symbolic of the cities and suburban areas to which the women would shortly return.

Photographer: Olive Edis
Source: IWM Q8120

PLATE 118 *Opposite*
WRNS Ratings storewomen sorting ships' lamps at Lowestoft, summer 1918

It is possibly because the many items of naval equipment sorted and stored by the WRNS are in themselves attractive and evocative objects that photographs such as this are so appealing. Certainly the kerchiefed figures of the girls posed against the light-refracting lamps has a limpid Vermeer-like quality perhaps sought after by the photographer.

Photographer: G. P. Lewis
Source: IWM Q9733

PLATE 119 *Opposite, top*
Ratings of the Women's Royal Naval Service, *HMS Victory*, Crystal Palace, Sydenham, 1918

The original caption to this photograph is 'Types of WRNS Ratings'. These four girls, two of whom were clerical workers, one a storekeeper, porter or messenger, and the fourth not yet in receipt of her category badge, did their initial training at the Crystal Palace which had been requisitioned by the Admiralty as a vast training depot for the RNVR. It is interesting to note that the rating second from the left is wearing a plain collar. The traditional sailor's collar of blue with the three white lines was not at first allowed to the WRNS, although so many girls obtained these coveted symbols from their sailor boyfriends that the plain collar was quickly abandoned and the blue and white one introduced. Except for one motor-boat on the south coast, and work on board ships in harbour, the WRNS never went to sea; their role was to replace on land men who could go to sea and fight.

Photographer: Unknown
Source: IWM Q18897

PLATE 120 *Opposite, bottom*
Dame Katherine Furse GBE, Director WRNS, and her Secretary, Miss M. Butcher MBE, 1918

Katherine Furse, widowed at the early age of 29 and left with two young children by her husband the painter Charles W. Furse ARA, joined the newly formed Voluntary Aid Detachment in 1910. In 1914 she went to France with some of the first detachments to serve with the BEF, returning later to London to set up the VAD Headquarters at Devonshire House (shared with the first of the Women's Services, the WAAC). In June 1917 she was amongst the first list of women to be gazetted to membership of the First Class of the newly instituted Order of the British Empire. By that time, however, she had become increasingly disillusioned with the internal wranglings within the Joint War Committee of the BRCS and the Order of St John, and resigned from her post in November 1917. In that same month she had a meeting with Sir Eric Geddes (brother of Mrs Chalmers Watson of the WAAC), with a view to setting up a uniformed organisation for women to work with the Navy. The new service just escaped being called the Women's Auxiliary Naval Corps, but the name Women's Royal Naval Service was finally agreed. Dame Katherine took with her from the VAD/BRCS a number of colleagues, including Miss Butcher. On 29 November 1917 the WRNS came into being officially with the publication of the Admiralty Office Memorandum (No. 245). The first officers were trained with the help of the WAAC, and, while later the WRNS achieved a particularly good working relationship with the Royal Navy, there were 'old salts' who did not welcome the innovation. 'Of all the 'orrible things this 'orrible war has done, these 'orrible women are the worst,' one Chief Petty Officer is recorded as saying. Dame Katherine, as Director, worked to the Second Sea Lord and soon moved offices from Devonshire House to 15 Great Stanhope Street, close to the Admiralty. Dame Katherine, something of a 'Bohemian' who had spent much of her youth living abroad, was far from self-effacing, and it is clear that a woman with so formidable a reputation did not feel constrained to imitate masculine austerity in her own office. As has been stated before, women of all ranks took any opportunity, as here, to surround themselves with flowers, and personal pictures and objects.

Photographer: G. P. Lewis
Source: IWM Q9733

PLATE 121
Recreation room at the WRNS Quarters, Osea Island, summer 1918

Women serving alongside men in the Services had strictly limited opportunities for social contact with them. Still, for their off-duty entertainment these WRNS appear to have been reasonably well equipped, since they had not only a piano but a gramophone as well. The room is rather spartan, but even the apparently inadequate stove could be cheered up, at least in summer, by the addition of some flowers in what looks very like a service-issue enamel jug.

Photographer: G. P. Lewis
Source: IWM Q19746

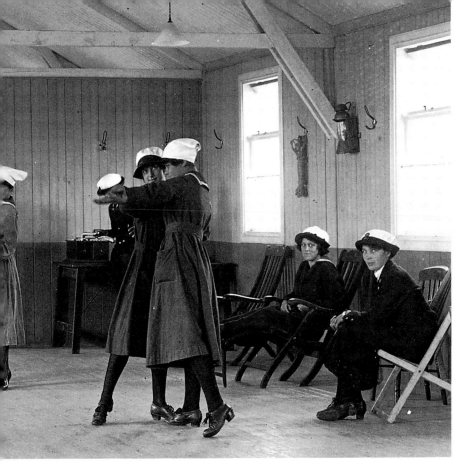

PLATE 122
**WRNS Record Office,
Stanhope Gate, London 1918**

As might be expected, Admiral Lord Nelson, in the guise of an exhortation to buy war bonds, looks benignly down on the WRNS Clerks at the Headquarters Office at Stanhope Gate. Here WRNS maintained the records of the day-to-day activities of the service, ratings working side-by-side with Principals. There is something rather charmingly innocent about the collection of china figures on the mantelpiece, and again there are vases of flowers. The WRNS seem to have been a particularly successful service, avoiding many of the teething troubles suffered by the WAAC and the especial difficulties brought about by interservice rivalry which bedevilled the foundation of the WRAF.

Photographer: G. P. Lewis
Source: IWM Q19690

PLATE 123 *Previous page*

Members of the Women's Royal Air Force boarding Air Force tenders to go to their billets in Cologne, 19 May 1919

The Royal Air Force was formed as a result of the merging of the two air arms, the Royal Flying Corps and the Royal Naval Air Service. The new Service drew its officers and men from both of the old flying services, and its uniform (at first khaki, then light blue, and finally the familiar grey blue) and badges were a curious mixture of the Army and the Royal Navy. The Women's Royal Air Force also drew its personnel from the WAAC and those members of the WRNS who served on the Royal Naval Air Stations, but unlike its parent service, whose birth was relatively painless, the WRAF suffered desperate difficulties before it finally emerged as the smart disciplined Service whose members went with the Army of Occupation to Germany in 1919. 45 officers and 2,821 ratings came from the WRNS; 67 officers and 6,738 other ranks from the WAAC and 496 drivers from the Women's Legion. From the start women in the WRAF were more closely integrated into the new Service than their opposite numbers in the WRNS and the WAAC. This was in part due to the fact that the RAF was a pioneer service and both men and women were equally welcome so long as they were what was then known as 'air minded'. The WRAF moved to Cologne with the Headquarters in the Field of the RAF, where 14 officers and 341 other ranks were to serve. The WRAF left Cologne on 1 November 1919. Despite the hope that the new Service would survive the coming of peace, the WRAF was finally disbanded by 1 April 1920. It was the last Service to be founded and the last to be disbanded.

Photographer: Unknown
Source: IWM Q7642

PLATE 124 *Opposite*

WAAC Drivers attending to the engine of an officer's car, Abbéville, 15 September 1917

Large numbers of WAACs served at the Advanced Mechanical Transport Depot which was situated at Abbéville. They not only ran the stores, and organised the paperwork which kept hundreds of the Army's motor vehicles on the road, but they also drove the cars, and carried out some of the basic day-to-day servicing. Motor transport might have been the latest in technological innovation, but other resources were still very basic: the women are using a leather bucket to hold water for cleaning the car.

Photographer: Unknown
Source: IWM Q5956

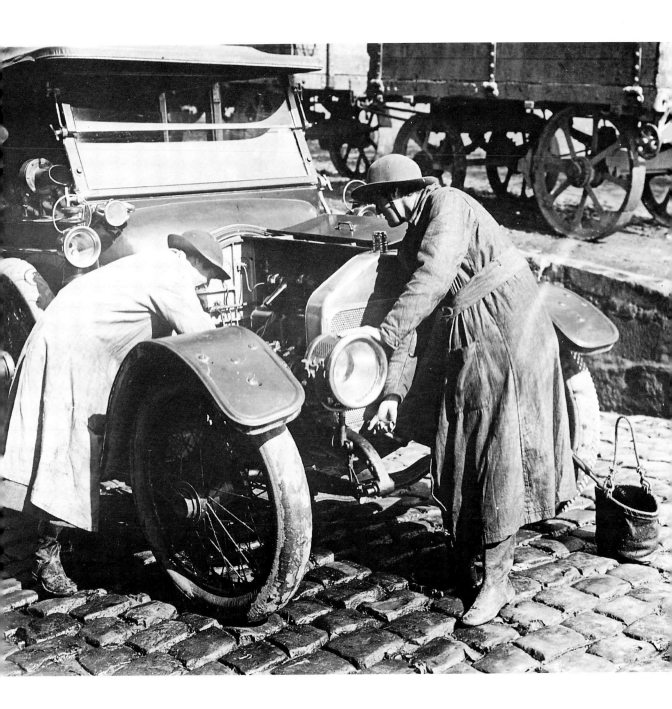

PLATE 125

**Women Air Mechanics of the
Women's Royal Air Force
working on the fuselage of
the AVRO 540, probably
1919**

The location of this
photograph is not known, but
the aircraft, the AVRO 540,
was a post-war gunnery
trainer version of the AVRO
504K. From the very
beginning the WRAF were
encouraged to take a real
interest in the machines for
which the new Service
existed. Officers and other
ranks were able to get air
experience and, whilst not
officially able to fly, could take
instruction. The disbanding of
the WRAF and the male
domination of post-war flying
effectively debarred women
from the development of
aviation in whose beginning
they had played so vital a
part. The seeds of their
involvement had been sown,
however, as the post-war
expansion of private flying
provided women such as
Amy Johnson with the
chance to fly on equal terms
with men.

Photographer: Unknown
Source: IWM Q27255

PLATE 126
Woman Motor Driver serving with the Royal Flying Corps, *c.* autumn 1917

The Royal Flying Corps which had been formed in 1912 was the air arm of the Army, with a dashing image enhanced by the unique uniform worn by its members. Military aviation was still in its infancy, but was to prove a vital element during the First World War. Women did not serve in the RFC, although Women's Legion drivers were attached to the corps, wearing the shoulder flash and brass cap badge. The uniform was khaki, and was a smart gaberdine jacket and skirt. The collar and tie leave something to be desired, but the splendid driving gauntlets finish off the outfit and convey a dashing carefree image. Women serving with the RFC were eventually absorbed into the WAAC, and then into the newly formed Royal Air Force which was born on 1 April 1918. The 'Broad Arrow' stencilled on to the windscreen surround indicates that the car is official government property.

Photographer: Unknown
Source: IWM Q33817

PLATE 127
Women's Royal Air Force Clerk, 1919

The image of the new Service is well exemplified in this portrait of a WRAF Clerk with her puppy. The uniform was a light blue gaberdine, with white badges on a black backing. The buttons were brass with the Royal Air Force Eagle, and the shirt white with a black tie. The charm of the subject lies in the healthy open air quality created by the photographer, enhanced by the cuddly appeal of the puppy. Here in fact are the components of the post-war image of the desirable woman, which emphasised the outdoor, active, sport-loving girl rather than the delicate, elaborately dressed ladylike creation of the pre-war age.

Photographer: Unknown
Source: IWM Q12260P

PLATE 128 *Above*

Members of the Women's Forestry Corps stripping the bark off trees, Cross in Hand, Heathfield, Sussex, June 1918

The heavy ground covering of bark shavings suggests that this was the regular spot where the women undertook this work, so that Nicholls had a readymade backdrop for his idyllic view of women in the English countryside. This work was hard, but it was also pleasant to be in the open air in summer. The winter was another matter, and a small number of land workers did die from related illnesses. Timber was a vital commodity for the prosecution of the war: for fuel, for construction, for production of paper, for component parts of rifles, for the production of packing cases, containers such as ammunition boxes, and of course for duck boards in the trenches and wood to build the parapets. The demand for the raw material was enormous, and considerable areas of traditional woodland were felled in the name of the war effort. The WFC worked for the Timber Supply Department of the Board of Trade.

Photographer: Horace W. Nicholls
Source: IWM Q30704

PLATE 129 *Opposite*

Two members of the Women's Forestry Corps grinding an axe, Cross in Hand, Heathfield, Sussex, June 1918

Nicholls, whose work suggests that he had a keen eye for a pretty girl, has perfectly caught the popular image of working on the land. Despite the hard manual nature of the work, there is a delicacy and charm about this picture which must have done much to promote what was a very unglamorous job. These women are both young and the masculine nature of their clothes – the heavy corduroy breeches and the canvas smock – in fact enhances the traditional prettiness of their profiles, crowned by coils of hair. The girl on the right is certainly not wearing the regulation rough cotton blouse, and (like other women in these photographs) she has also managed to acquire a wristwatch. Until the First World War these were worn only by the military, fob watches being the usual civilian wear.

Photographer: Horace W. Nicholls
Source: IWM Q30719

PLATE 130

Women horse trainers, at Rimington's Establishment at Shrewsbury, October 1919. Nicholls's original caption for this picture was 'Lady Trainers getting Mules used to harness; a leader and wheelers get mixed up when in harness for the first time'

Mules were the pack animals of the British Army and thousands of them were used all over the world, hauling carts and carrying ammunition and stores. There were 'remount' depots in France where horses were broken and trained for use, but a considerable number of women were employed on this type of work at home, under the auspices of the Army Service Corps. For any young woman fond of horses, with the ability to ride or drive, the chance to work with them was much sought after. It wasn't without its dangers, however, and there were casualties, amongst whom was a daughter of Queen Mary's Lady-in-Waiting, the Countess of Airlie, who was killed as a result of a fall while exercising horses for the Army.

Photographer: Horace W. Nicholls
Source: IWM Q30926

PLATE 131
A woman horse trainer at Rimington's Establishment at Shrewsbury, October 1919, administering what Nicholls called 'the earclutch method to prevent escaping proclivities'

There seems to have been plenty of fun as well as hard work, but whether the mule was very amused is another matter. Women engaged in training horses rode astride as a matter of course (after all, no army officer would have ridden side-saddle), and were suitably attired in jodhpurs and boots. The uniform, like civilian riding clothes, was smart and serviceable.

Photographer: Horace W. Nicholls
Source: IWM Q30921

PLATE 132

Woman farm worker feeding poultry, possibly near Langstock, in Hampshire, 1918

Although women had not traditionally been employed in large numbers on the land as agriculture declined in the nineteenth century, the female relatives of the farmer, or farm hands, were usually employed to look after the poultry. Indeed the hens, and the income produced from the sale of eggs, were always regarded as being the perk of the farmer's wife or daughter. This stunning photograph, which seems to owe much to English watercolourists of the nineteenth century, manages to create the fairytale world which illustrators such as Arthur Rackham so memorably evoked out of such elements as the cottage secretively hidden by overhanging hedgerows.

Photographer: Horace W. Nicholls
Source: IWM Q31136

PLATE 133 *Above*
Members of the Women's Forage Corps feeding a hay baler. A party of six girls and a sergeant of the Army Service Corps form the working complement of a baler, Middlesex, summer 1918

The function of the Women's Forage Corps, which came under the control of the Army Service Corps and therefore the War Office, was to provide forage for the Army's use. This was hard dusty work, and obviously not made any pleasanter by the smoke belching from the steam engine driving the baler. The introduction of new technology made this work a feasible proposition for women, but it is of interest to note, and important in keeping a sense of proportion where women's contribution to the land is concerned, that of the total numbers working on the land during the war years, only one-third were women. The other two-thirds were German prisoners of war, and soldiers who, the ASC apart, were regularly employed to bring in the harvest and help out generally on the land near their camps or garrison towns.

Photographer: Horace W. Nicholls
Source: IWM Q30691

PLATE 134 *Oposite*
Members of the Women's Land Army starting out for work, Dens Farm, Harefield, nr Uxbridge, Middlesex, probably the summer of 1918

A full-time regulated and paid workforce was to prove to be the answer to some of the problems which the many part-time, voluntary groups working on the land had failed to solve. In February 1917 one of the most famous of the women's wartime organisations came into being with the formation of the Women's Land Army (WLA). With the new corps, the Forestry Corps became separated from the WLA, the former remaining under the control of the Board of Trade, and the latter coming under the control of the Board of Agriculture and Fisheries. Over 113,000 women served on the land during the First World War. The appeal of the open-air life was strong for many town dwellers, and the romantic notion of the bountiful countryside, and warm idyllic summer days, was as hard to resist then as it is now; the image of healthy, happy workers doing a vital job in beautiful surroundings is well captured here by Nicholls. These girls are fortunate in that they had fellow landgirls on the same farm. This was by no means always the case, and for some, alone on small farms, with perhaps only an old farmworker who might well resent their presence, and the farmer's wife who perhaps disapproved, as did many women, of their 'apeing' of men in their masculine dress, it was a grim and weary way to spend the war.

Photographer: Horace W. Nicholls
Source: IWM Q30669

PLATE 135 *Left*
WLA member watering her horses, Dens Farm, 1918

This was clearly the horses' regular watering hole, judging by the muddy ground churned up in the foreground. This image is timeless and again (like Plate 132) relates to a deeply ingrained English tradition of the pastoral. Because of this Nicholls appears to tap the same sources in these photographs as did the artist John Constable in his early nineteenth-century landscape paintings. Women have often been perceived as having a special relationship with horses, and this emerges from Nicholls's composition. Like the good cavalryman who cares for his horse before himself, this WLA girl made certain her horses received their refreshment before she took her own.

Photographer: Horace W. Nicholls
Source: IWM Q30667

PLATE 136 *Above*
Women's Land Army member with a team of horses ploughing, Dens Farm, Harefield, nr Uxbridge, Middlesex, 1918

Women had not traditionally worked the plough horses, but the war changed that and gave them the opportunity to try their hand at what was one of the most skilled jobs on the land. The ground looks dry and hard, and the horses far from the traditionally handsome heavyweight shires. Indeed, the poor animals whilst obviously cared for – their coats clean, and their ears covered to protect them against the incessant worrying of the horse fly – are painfully thin. So proficient did some women become at ploughing that in many parts of the country they happily demonstrated their ability in traditional ploughing matches where they did extremely well.

Photographer: Horace W. Nicholls
Source: IWM Q30658

PLATE 137
Women's Forestry Corps member in uniform, April 1918

This was one of a series of photographs of women in uniform, taken by Horace Nicholls at the Queen Anne's Gate offices of the Women's Work Section of the Imperial War Museum. The idea was to record for posterity the various uniforms worn by women, and by implication the many organisations to which they had belonged. This is a smart businesslike uniform, of heavy khaki drill working coat, brown leather belt, brown leather lace-up boots and gaiters, collar and tie, and rather cheerful looking beret with the WFC badge. The breeches were light tan corduroy, and while very smart and hard wearing, were found to be desperately uncomfortable by many of those who wore them, one of the main problems being that the heavy inside seams were rough and unfinished.

Photographer: Horace W. Nicholls
Source: IWM Q30614

PLATE 138
Women forestry workers, Cross in Hand, Heathfield, Sussex, with logs loaded on to a sledge for transportation to the stacks, June 1918

These well-fed horses provide a marked contrast to the pair drawing the plough in Plate 136. Felling and trimming timber is of course a skilled and dangerous job. The women were supervised by an experienced male forestry worker, who like many of the men working with female colleagues at that time, was well over age for military service.

Photographer: Horace W. Nicholls
Source: IWM Q106565

PLATE 139 *Above*
Princess Mary picking fruit in Frogmore Gardens, watched by Queen Mary, September 1917

Fruit growing was vital for bottling and jam-making at a period when commercially tinned and preserved foods were still not widely available. Fruit picking in fact was one of the first wartime tasks that brought women back to the land. As food shortages increased later in the war home-grown fruit became even more important. Here the Queen and Princess Mary are making a private contribution to the public war effort.

Photographer: Unknown
Source: Royal Archives, Queen Mary's Photograph Albums

PLATE 140 *Right*
Typical girl flax puller, Barwick, 1918

The Women's Farm and Garden Union was the only existing organisation which dealt with women's work on the land before the war. The Women's National Land Service Corps was launched in February 1916 as a wartime offshoot of this society by Mrs Roland Wilkins OBE. During the war the corps placed 9,022 women on the land and acted as agent for the Women's Branch of the Board of Agriculture in placing holiday workers from other parts of the country. In 1918, this worker with over 3,835 of her fellows, who were mainly college students, saved the flax harvest from ruin. Flax was an immensely important product, because linen was much in demand for such diverse purposes as clothing and making covers for shell charges. Once more Nicholls has responded to the familiar pastoral image of a pretty girl binding sheaves in a rural setting.

Photographer: Horace W. Nicholls
Source: IWM Q30887

PLATE 141

Woman window cleaner employed by the Mayfair Window Cleaning Co. Ltd, 1918

Cleaning the windows of a draper's shop might not be the popular public idea of heroism, nor would some believe that such an activity made any great contribution to the war effort. Both views have some validity, but of course neither really grasp the significance of the image which this photograph conveys. Women were prepared to carry the skills which they utilised in their own domestic sphere out into the employment market created by the war and in doing so made their contribution, however mundane the work. If the work was not especially heroic the spirit which the women brought to it can in some measure be described as such. Cleaning, one of the most basic and important of the domestic chores, was a skill which women practised in virtually every sphere, expanding their long-established abilities into transport, and the public utilities. The work may have remained much the same, but the image of the women engaged in it was changed irrevocably by the war.

Photographer: G. P. Lewis
Source: IWM Q28032

CHAPTER VI

FROM HOUSEWIFE TO HEROINE

'Votes for Heroines as Well as Heroes'
(Slogan from *Votes For Women* 26 November 1915)

By 1918 the restrictive Victorian image of womanhood – physically frail, sheltered, leisured, private – had been undermined by the wartime experience of both sexes. It was now permissible for women to be physically courageous, enduring, responsible, conscientious, cheerful and outgoing. They assumed responsibility in skilled jobs, endured physical hardship, mastered control of new technology, were financially independent through reasonable wages and obtained the right to join male trade unions. Many women had witnessed the suffering and anguish of men as they had not in previous wars, and had also worked side-by-side with men as comrades and friends. It was inevitable that this would start to change mutual perceptions, and the granting of the vote at last (to women over 30) seemed entirely appropriate. Such women now had a direct political stake in the future they had helped to secure.

Although, following the end of the war, some long-term prospects in new areas of employment had opened up, notably in transport and clerical work, most women lost their jobs as the men returned. The problems of peace seemed more intractable than the problems of war. Men and women who had complemented each other in the war effort now found themselves in competition for jobs in a rapidly shrinking economy; both sexes were likely to find themselves unemployed.

Having achieved in wartime a new and more public relationship with the state, with society, and with men, women in peacetime found that the urgency had gone, and they were now being pushed back into the private sphere. War after all was seen as an abnormal and temporary state, the women's role in it was viewed in the same light. There was as well a general reaction against public control of private affairs, symptomatic of a longing for the familiarity of the pre-war world. Women too felt the pull of private life, and the pleasures of marriage and children; this conveniently coincided with the beginnings of a general economic recession.

For many women, however, there was no possibility of a return to their pre-war life. Thousands had lost fathers, husbands, sons, brothers and fiancés, and had to carry on making their own way in difficult circumstances. It was these women who maintained a presence outside the domestic sphere, and thus ensured that the potential revealed by women in the First World War was never entirely forgotten.

PLATE 142

Women railway carriage cleaner using a vacuum cleaner, London terminus, 1918

Women engaged on this type of work during the First World War at least had the benefit of advances in the design and production of domestic and industrial appliances. These appliances did much to make the work easier and quicker, although it was still hard and the conditions far from pleasant.

Photographer: Unknown
Source: IWM Q109879

PLATE 143
Woman gas lamp cleaner on the railways, 1918

It is not known just how many gas lamps this worker had to clean, but it is possible to imagine a long line of these incongruously elegant lamps; there is a bleak solitude about this woman perched on the iron step ladder, cloth in right hand and wire brush in the left. The photographer has managed to invest her, in her humble and disregarded task, with a certain indomitable quality, silhouetted against the sky and misty Victorian townscape.

Photographer: Unknown
Source: IWM Q109866

PLATE 144
Women labourers employed by the Lancashire and Yorkshire Railway, Manchester, cleaning the glass on the roof of Clifton Power Station, 15 May 1917

Fourteen women were employed on this work which, like many cleaning jobs, was unending; no sooner had they finished than off they had to go again. There is no sign of a hose pipe, presumably because the glass would have been liable to breakage if high pressure hoses had been used, so these women resorted to buckets and mops. This was clearly no job for someone afraid of heights. When they went back to being housewives and later, when their grandchildren asked them what they had done in the Great War, the answer 'I cleaned the glass roof of Clifton Power Station' must have raised a few eyebrows. This is a marvellous image with the small figures high up on the power station roof in the hazy sunshine.

Photographer: Unknown
Source: IWM Q109860

PLATE 145
Women glass workers in Lancashire in the sludge pits treating the residue from the sand-working tables, 1918

Before the First World War women were no strangers to either hardship or responsibility, although in most instances these privations were within the domestic sphere. With the outbreak of war and their introduction into so many of the manufacturing processes, women began to experience a new form of hardship with filthy working conditions, dangerous industrial processes and hard, backbreaking work. They left that only to go home to more familiar demands of their duties as wife, mother or daughter in a society where, for the most part, their men were absent and responsibilities now devolved upon them. These women at least had the benefit of suitable waterproof boots, headgear and overalls to protect them.

Photographer: G. P. Lewis
Source: IWM Q28397

PLATE 146
Girls packing electric light bulbs at a factory in Birmingham, *c.* 1918

The composition and lighting of this photograph is remarkable, even to the highlighting on the glass bulbs. The image is gentle, virginal and almost impossibly romantic. The straw packing materials on the floor suggest a country barn, but outside in the sunshine are the roofs of adjacent buildings which put this picture firmly in the centre of industrial England. Recycling boxes was obviously in vogue; the St Bruno tobacco crate carried by the girl standing by the door must have been a weight, and the consequences of dropping it disastrous.

Photographer: G. P. Lewis
Source: IWM Q28172

PLATE 147 *Above*
Woman attendant employed in a bacteriological laboratory located in the works of Messrs Lyle & Co., 1918

The pre-war and early-war image of women, as portrayed in photographs, is romantic and reassuring; fulfilling their traditional roles, and looking appropriately demure and attractive whilst doing so, as with nursing. By the time the war was into its advanced stages, the image of women engaged in war work had begun to change; they were competent and skilled and, above all, their work was seen as being directed towards a purpose: the pursuit of victory, the triumph of good over evil. If women became less romanticised, less 'feminine' through adopting more masculine ways, then that was perceived as acceptable as long as the end, victory, justified the wholesale involvement of women and the inevitable sacrifice of the earlier 'feminine' image. But there were those who saw that it was possible to combine the two; for women not only to be seen as having skills, having a purpose, and being part of the concept of a nation in arms; and yet still be romanticised. This young woman is obviously competent and professional. She is pretty and 'feminine' in an unfeminine environment – yet the photograph is softly lit, romantically posed, and, test tubes and Bunsen burners notwithstanding, it could be the image of a young girl seated in her boudoir. Her professional skills have not, in this image, made her alarmingly unfamiliar.

Photographer: Unknown
Source: IWM Q106592

PLATE 148 *Opposite*
**Woman railway worker operating signals in a cabin on a siding, Great Central Railway, Birmingham,
September 1918**

Any form of work in the transport system on which other people's lives depended demanded a degree of
responsibility and skill which few believed women possessed. The war soon disproved this notion for when
a woman showed she had a responsible and sensible approach to her job the opportunities were there, if only
for the duration of the war. This woman, though not especially young, looks smart, competent, and physically
capable.

Photographer: G. P. Lewis
Source: IWM Q28148

PLATE 149 *Above*
A woman motor lorry driver employed by Glasgow Tramways Department, July 1917

Driving a lorry for the Tramways Department in Glasgow meant a working week of 56 hours, as well as full
responsibility for the vehicle and the safety of other road users. It also meant a sense of duty and responsibility
to turn out on time every day, and to undertake this unglamorous work without the more public recognition
which the uniformed services attracted.

Photographer: Unknown
Source: IWM Q110169

PLATE 150 *Previous page, top left*
Women workers tar-spraying a London street, probably 1918

This image is direct, simple and curiously appealing. Women's working conditions had always been hard, and their chances to develop real skills, which if used would better their living standards, very limited. The heavy buckled wooden 'clogs', covered in tar, the overalls spattered with the stuff, and the all-pervading smell which must have clung in the hair and nose, were an unpleasant but inevitable consequence of this work. Women working on the streets doing this kind of manual labour would have been unthinkable before the war, but by 1917 it had become commonplace and the women who did this work made their own very special contribution to victory. The sight of women undertaking road repair work, even now, would undoubtedly still shock some.

Photographer: Horace W. Nicholls
Source: IWM Q30876

PLATE 151 *Previous, bottom left*
Members of the women's Fire Brigade at a Middlesex munitions factory, January 1918

The notion that women could be useful and responsible members of an organisation such as the Fire Brigade would have been quite unthinkable before the large-scale exodus of men to the Army, but women did learn the skills of this new job. While there were no prospects of similar employment after the war, (indeed it is extremely doubtful whether women would have wanted to be so employed), women performed the tasks allotted to them with courage, responsibility and an enjoyment of the hitherto unfamiliar experience of *esprit de corps*.

Photographer: Unknown
Source: IWM Q108478

PLATE 152 *Previous page, right*
Woman granite worker employed on sand-blasting at Messrs Stewart & Co. Ltd, Fraser Place, Aberdeen, Scotland, September 1918

It is difficult not to see in this image of a woman sand-blaster a parallel with the gas-helmeted troops on the Western Front. Normal industries had to be maintained, and despite the hard and unpleasant conditions (the heat must have been awful in the summer) it was women who largely managed to keep the wheels of these non-essential, but money-earning industries, going. Here any gesture towards traditional femininity would be absurd. It would seem that Lewis deliberately presented his subject as a sexless image inside a protective uniform pointing a 'weapon' at a tombstone. The granite slab with its Celtic cross is clearly a gravestone laid horizontally.

Photographer: G. P. Lewis
Source: IWM Q28376

PLATE 153 *Following page*
Mrs Gerard Barnes, WRNS motor-boat driver, with her dog, Southwick, Sussex, June 1918

The war provided many new opportunities for women of all classes, and, while in many spheres they were only able to lay the groundwork for the next generation, one of the lasting changes which the Great War wrought was in the image which women had of themselves and which was offered to others. They had shown themselves to be prepared to turn their hand to anything: suffer hardship, accept responsibility, and yet, against many expectations, they had managed to retain their traditional femininity. But the war had added a new dimension to how women saw themselves, and their relationship with other women as well as men. In addition to the expected virtues, women could now claim to be not merely decorative, or pretty, but plucky, cheerful, competent, trustworthy and fully conversant with such important public concepts as honour and duty. The war was an education in more ways than one and if the new jobs which women had done in the war were closed to them afterwards, the other opportunities, conveyed by their new image, were not. Women could play a fuller role, and enjoy their new-found self-confidence. This photograph shows an active, cheerful, competent young woman. The White Ensign and the uniform denote the public effort and duty to the state. The pet dog (wet from a dip in the sea) reveals the private commitment to the world of personal relationships.

Photographer: G. P. Lewis
Source: IWM Q19727

PLATE 154
Woman railway porter on the London South Eastern & Chatham Railway with two calves, *c.* 1917

Managing these young calves formed part of the varied work of women on the railways. The young woman porter, in her smart, but obviously well-worn uniform, looks as though she knows exactly what she's doing, and needs no help from anyone; nor has she mislaid her sense of humour. Such a photograph when seen in a newspaper by the men at the front would no doubt have raised a few laughs and some ribald comments, but the point would not have been lost – women were getting on with the job of running things in the absence of their men, and were managing well.

Photographer: Unknown
Source: IWM Q110104

PLATE 155
A Forestry Corps Forewoman with her two children, Cross in Hand, Heathfield, Sussex, June 1918

By 1918 women were visibly engaged in virtually every area of working life. One of the major changes which this new involvement brought was in the publicly acceptable image of women. The passive Victorian notion of sheltered womanhood was now antiquated and old fashioned. Voluminous skirts and whalebone had gone for good, and practical clothes as shown here were the order of the day. With these practical clothes and more publicly active lives emerged the qualities now found admirable in women. They had always possessed courage, endurance, responsibility, cheerfulness and patriotism, but these had been submerged in private concerns; with the chance to shine, women had found a new self-confidence. Yet women themselves accepted generally that the war effort was temporary, and were ambivalent about keeping jobs needed by out-of-work ex-servicemen. Women in agriculture and forestry, like this one, would almost all lose their jobs, and few would find a means outside the domestic sphere for the opportunities of self-expression and self-fulfilment which the war had given them. There was of course another factor for many hundreds of thousands of women to consider. Their men would not be coming home, and they faced the future probably without work, with all the responsibilities of coping alone, and in many cases bringing up their children without a father so that the qualities which they had shown in war would be needed in peace. In this situation, these women who now had to cope on their own received one reward at least; if they were over 30 and householders on 6 February 1918, they got the long-awaited vote.

Photographer: Horace W. Nicholls
Source: IWM Q30696

PLATE 156
Olive Edis Galsworthy, known as Olive Edis, 1876–1955

Olive Edis was the only woman photographer to be commissioned by the Women's Work Sub-Committee of the Imperial War Museum to record the work of the Women's Services in France and Flanders. Although the Armistice was signed in November 1918, the war was not officially ended until the Treaty of Versailles of 1919, and the cadres of the Women's Services, like the Armed Forces, remained abroad until then to wind down the war effort. It was in March 1919 that Olive Edis made her tour of the battle fronts. She herself was the daughter of an architect and had taken up photography in 1900, opening studios in Norfolk, Surrey and later in London. Her photographic work included portraits of many notable figures of the time, including Emmeline Pankhurst and Elizabeth Garrett Anderson, as well as John Galsworthy whose cousin she married. She became a Fellow of the Royal Photographic Society in 1914. This self-portrait shows her not only with her camera but wearing a uniform enlivened by a necklace. Her stylish image clearly impressed those she met; to Agnes Conway of the Women's Work Sub-Committee she reported on 31 October 1918 '... They ask me if my badge means New Woman's Movement' (File IWMCF A/WW 5A/4 'Visits'). In fact her cap badge – NWM – stood for National War Museum.

Photographer: Olive Edis
Source: NPG Ref Neg no. 3015

PLATE 157
'Palmer Munitionettes', the women's football team made up of employees of the Palmers Shipbuilding Co. Ltd, Hebburn-on-Tyne, 1918

Quite apart from job opportunities, the war gave many women new openings where their leisure and social life were concerned. The chance to play in 'team' games, hitherto the preserve of men, or girls who had attended the grammar and public schools, was provided by the large numbers of young women whose work imbued them with a new sense of being part of a wider society. While cricket had always had a following amongst women, with a fair number of female players, and lacrosse, hockey and netball were played in schools, Association Football had never been thought a suitable game for women. It would be wrong to imply that sights such as these girls from Palmers were to be found all over the country. Indeed the fact that they were thought worthy of a photograph suggests that they were a rare event, but that they did exist, shorts, knees showing and by contemporary standards, in a rather immodest pose, can be seen as an indication of things to come. This team, three members short, were very competent, and took one of the factory nurses with them wherever they played in case of injury. The girls seem ready to take on all-comers, although the player on the extreme left in the front row looks rather less at home with her new-found freedom than do her team mates.

Photographer: Unknown
Source: IWM Q110074

PLATE 158
Off-duty members of the WAAC going down to bathe at Paris Plage, 25 July 1917

It is in the nature of warfare that most of those involved are young, full of high spirits, and resilient, so that given the opportunity they will find their entertainment and enjoyment despite the privations and the inevitable sadness. Indeed, such pleasures as sea bathing, dancing and other entertainments had their enjoyment heightened by the proximity of war. Modesty forbade a walk to the beach clad only in their bathing dresses, and the WAAC Administrator in uniform on the right is there to chaperone the girls. As this and previous photographs show, physical recreation and sporting activities became much more available for women during the war, and this was one area that was not closed to them afterwards. Indeed, participation in sport grew during the 1920s, and became a permanently acceptable element in post-war ideals of the feminine.

Photographer: Unknown
Source: IWM Q5758

Source: IWM Q110104

PLATE 159
VAD Christmas entertainment, at Constance, Duchess of Westminster's Hospital, France, 1917

Entertainment for those in France was very much a matter of making the best of what was available. With so many people thrown together from diverse backgrounds theatrical and musical talent was bound to surface if the opportunity arose. These VADs must have greatly enjoyed the fun of taking part in a Christmas concert, for they were far from home, as were the men and women who made up the audience. Interestingly the young women in their theatrically saucy French maid outfits seem, with their pouts and beauty spots, to be sending up the traditional pre-war notions of feminine sex appeal.

Photographer: Unknown
Source: IWM Q108171

Photographer: Unknown
Source: IWM Q108171

PLATE 160 *Previous page*
WAACs and soldiers on the edge of a crater caused by an enemy bomb dropped in their camp during an air raid at Abbéville, 22 May 1918

No women were killed in this particular raid, although several were injured and only four of the seventeen huts which accommodated the WAACs escaped destruction. Eight days later it was a different story. A German bomb hit a covered trench in which WAACs were sleeping, and eight were killed outright, whilst one died later of wounds and six others were wounded. As a result of their coolness and courage under fire four women were awarded the Military Medal. There were mercifully few deaths of women as a direct result of enemy action in France and Belgium, although there were deaths from illness, disease and accidents. These deaths in action did have a profound effect upon the WAACs, and upon the men with whom they served. The dead were buried on 31 May will full military honours. As the coffins, followed by members of the WAAC and army officers, were carried to the gravesides, almost every soldier in the camp left their billets and offices to salute as the gun carriages went by, and overhead the Royal Air Force circled to protect the area whilst the women were buried. For soldiers death is an occupational hazard. Yet, however much the women who served with them wanted to be part of the Army and serve their King and Country, the society from which they came did not see it as appropriate that women should be placed in a situation where their lives were put at risk. For the women who were killed, and for those who witnessed their deaths, it cannot have been how they perceived their equality with men, and there is no doubt that few of the men who were there would have wanted it that way.

Photographer: Unknown
Source: IWM Q7890

PLATE 161
WAACs tending the graves of British soldiers in a cemetery, Abbéville, 9 February 1918

In peacetime death is a private matter, and a public display of grief rarely extends beyond the immediate circle of the deceased. In war death is public, and sorrow at the loss of so many lives permeates the whole of society. The sheer weight of numbers in the First World War makes it very difficult to comprehend the nature of the grief of those whose husbands, fathers, sons, brothers and friends were killed. It became a matter of immense importance that the individual nature of death and the uniqueness of each life lost should not be submerged by the statistics. The work of the Graves Registration Service (which became the Imperial and later Commonwealth War Graves Commission) is beyond the scope of this book, but this photograph, taken when the arrangement of the war cemeteries was beginning to take place, illustrates in a very simple and moving way the intensely personal nature of the losses. It was the job of these WAACs to tend the graves, and to make sure that simple wreaths, sent by families and friends were placed on the appropriate graves.

Photographer: Unknown
Source: IWM Q8471

PLATE 162 *Opposite*
Women munition workers in Swansea mourning the death of a colleague killed in an accident at work, August Bank Holiday 1917

Apart from those casualties from enemy action in France and Belgium, and the German air raids on England, the most obvious measure of how women's situations had been changed by the war were the deaths from causes directly attributable to war work. Munitions work was dangerous, and there were bound to be accidents, however much care was taken to guard against them. This woman's sacrifice in a factory on the Home Front was no less than that of the soldier cut down on the Somme or the sailor drowned at sea. This outpouring of grief for one unknown woman may seem to our eyes excessive, yet the shock and sorrow manifest on the faces of these women says a great deal about the sense of common humanity which managed to survive in an age of total war where women were participants as they had never been before.

Photographer: Unknown
Source: IWM Q108452

PLATE 163 *Over*
WAAC gardeners tending the graves of war dead, Etaples, March 1919

Olive Edis took this photograph on her tour with Agnes Conway and Lady Norman in the first winter after the war. Already the rows of graves are beginning to take on a uniform appearance and, within a few years, the wooden crosses would be replaced by white headstones. Soon the rows of graves would be set amongst green grass, trees, flowers and shrubs, and Lutyens's monuments to the thousands of dead would mark the old lines of the British advances in France and Flanders. Women would count the cost of the war in many ways, not the least of those being the shortage of men of marriageable age, the loss of the opportunity of a home and family, and the prospect of unemployment. In the face of death, these losses may not seem much, and indeed few would dispute that women, in the long term, gained more than they lost. But it is arguable that those gains, which included the vote, were won not for the generation of women who were adult during the First World War, but for those who were to face the Second World War, the young schoolgirls and children who in the years 1914–1918 had learnt from the example of their mothers, aunts, grandmothers and older sisters.

Photographer: Olive Edis
Source: IWM Q8027

ABBREVIATIONS

ACD	Army Clothing Department
ACI	Army Council Instruction
AEF	American Expeditionary Force
APMMC	Almeric Paget Military Massage Corps
ASC	Army Service Corps
BEF	British Expeditionary Force
BRCS	British Red Cross Society
CMO	Chief Medical Officer
DoI	Department of Information
DORA	Defence of the Realm Act
FANY	First Aid Nursing Yeomanry
GBE	Knight or Dame Grand Cross of the Most Excellent Order of The British Empire
GHQ	General Headquarters
HMS	His (Her) Majesty's Ship
IWM	Imperial War Museum
LCC	London County Council
MBE	Member of the Most Excellent Order of the British Empire
MO	Medical Officer
MoI	Ministry of Information
NCO	Non-Commissioned Officer
NPG	National Portrait Gallery
NSFF	National Shell Filling Factory
NUWSS	National Union of Women's Suffrage Societies
NUWW	National Union of Women Workers
OBE	Officer of the Most Excellent Order of The British Empire
O St J	Order of St John of Jerusalem
QAIMNS	Queen Alexandra's Imperial Military Nursing Service
QAIMNS(R)	Queen Alexandra's Imperial Military Nursing Service (Reserve)
QMAAC	Queen Mary's Army Auxiliary Corps (see WAAC)
QMNG	Queen Mary's Needlework Guild
QWWF	Queen's Work for Women Fund
RAF	Royal Air Force
RFC	Royal Flying Corps
RMA	Royal Marine Artillery
RN	Royal Navy
RNAS	Royal Naval Air Service (Royal Naval Air Station)
RNVR	Royal Naval Volunteer Reserve
ROF	Royal Ordnance Factory

RPS	Royal Photographic Society
RRC	Royal Red Cross
SWFAC	Scottish Women's First Aid Corps
SWH	Scottish Women's Hospitals
TF	Territorial Force
TFNS	Territorial Force Nursing Service
VAD	Voluntary Aid Detachment
WAAC	Women's Army Auxiliary Corps (in 1918 re-named Queen Mary's Army Auxiliary Corps but the old name retained in every day use)
WAF	Women's Auxiliary Force
WCC	Women's Convoy Corps
WDRC	Women's Defence Relief Corps
WEC	Women's Emergency Corps
WFC	Women's Forage Corps
WFC	Women's Forestry Corps
WHC	Women's Hospital Corps
WI	Women's Institute
WL	Women's Legion
WLA	Women's Land Army
WNLSC	Women's National Land Service Corps
WPS	Women's Police Service
WPV	Women's Police Volunteers
WRAF	Women's Royal Air Force
WRNS	Women's Royal Naval Service
WSPU	Women's Social and Political Union
WVR	Women's Vounteer Reserve

Year		Event
1898		National Union of Women's Suffrage Societies formed
1903		Women's Social and Political Union founded by the Pankhurst family
1907		First Aid Nursing Yeomanry (FANY) founded
1909		Women's Convoy Corps formed for Bulgarian wars by Mrs St Clair Stobart
1910		Voluntary Aid Detachment (VAD) set up
1910		Mrs Charlotte Despard breaks with WSPU to set up the Women's Freedom League
1912		Cat and Mouse Act passed
		Emily Wilding Davison of the WSPU throws herself under the King's horse at the Derby
1914	Feb	United Suffragists formed
	June 28	The Archduke Franz Ferdinand, heir to the Austro–Hungarian Empire, assassinated at Sarajevo, Serbia
	July 28	Austria–Hungary declares war on Serbia
	July 29	Russian government orders partial mobilization
	July 31	London Stock Exchange closed
	August 4	German troops cross Belgian border and attack Liège
		Britain declares war on Germany
		Mrs Millicent Garrett Fawcett, President of NUWSS, addresses Women's Protest Against War, London
	August 6	The Prince of Wales's National Relief Fund appeal launched
	August 7	First units of British Expeditionary Force land in France
	August 8 & 28	Defence of the Realm Act (DORA)
	August 20	German forces occupy Brussels
		Queen's Work For Women Fund launched
	August 21	British government issues order for raising of a 'new' army
	August 23	Battle of Mons
	August	Women's Emergency Corps set up
		Women's Interests' Committee set up
		Women's Volunteer Reserve set up
		Women's Defence Relief Corps set up
		Dr Hector Munro's Flying Ambulance Corps

		goes to Belgium accompanied by Elsie Knocker and Mairi Chisholm
		Central Committee on Women's Employment formed
	September 6	Battle of the Marne begins
	September 12	Battle of the Aisne
	September	Women's Hospital Corps set up
		Almeric Paget Military Massage Corps set up
		First woman bank teller employed by National Provincial and Union Bank of England Ltd
	October 29	National Union of Women Workers' Police Patrols officially recognised by the Home Office
	November	Women's Police Volunteers set up
		Atlas Assurance Co. Ltd employs women (other than as typists) to replace men
		Elsie Knocker and Mairi Chisholm set up First Aid Post at front line in village of Pervyse
	December	London Stock Exchange re-opens
1915	*January*	First Scottish Women's Hospital Unit goes to Kragujevac, Serbia under Dr Eleanor Soltau
	February 24	First Territorial Army units leave for France
	February	Women's Police Service set up
	March	Government Register of women willing to undertake agricultural, industrial and clerical work
	April	Glasgow Corporation employs first women tram conductors
	April 9	Leading Division of New Army leaves England for France
	May 7	Liner *Lusitania* torpedoed off southern Ireland
	May 25	Herbert Asquith as Prime Minister forms coalition
	May	Tramway Workers' Resolution (Manchester) against the employment of women
		Manchester women's suffragists establish Women's War Interests Committee to oversee women's conditions in munitions factories
	June	Sir William Beardmore's Engineering Works in Glasgow the first to employ skilled women workers in privately owned munitions factory
	July 2	Ministry of Munitions formed
	July 15	National Registration Act becomes law
	July 17	Women's Right to Serve March, London led by Emmeline and Christabel Pankhurst
	July 19	Lady Moir and Lady Cowan establish scheme for training ladies to undertake weekend work to relieve women workers at Vickers Armaments Factory, Erith, Kent
	July	Manchester and Salford Trades and Labour Council pass resolution opposing employment of women where men still available

		Women's Legion founded by Marchioness of Londonderry
	August 15	National Registration of all persons male and female between the ages of 15 and 25 years
	October 12	Edith Cavell shot in Brussels
	October 28	'L2' circular setting out women's wages for munitions workers
	November	Some crèches set up in factories for women workers from this time
		Home Office and Board of Trade establish Women's Employment Committee
	December 19	Sir Douglas Haig succeeds Sir John French as Commander-in-Chief, France
	December	Lilian Barker appointed Lady Superintendent, Royal Arsenal Woolwich
1915	*December*	Serbian retreat into Albania
1916	*January*	First Military Service Bill (conscription) passed
		Metropolitan Asylums Board Motor Ambulance Section employs women drivers
		Women's National Land Service Corps formed
	February	Army Council Instruction recognises Women's Legion
		Women's Forage Corps formed
	April 24	Outbreak of Irish Rebellion ('The Easter Rising')
	April 25	Lowestoft and Yarmouth raided by German battle cruiser squadron
	May 1	End of Irish Rebellion
	May 16	Conscription extended to married men
	May 17	Air Board formed
	May 25	Second Military Service Act becomes law
	July 1	Battle of the Somme begins
	July 23	Munitions Workers' Patriotic Procession
	July	London County Council Ambulance Corps employs entirely women
	December	WNLSC puts forward scheme for Women's Land Army
		Katherine Furse puts forward schemes for a women's military auxiliary corps
	December 4	Asquith resigns
	December 7	David Lloyd George becomes Prime Minister
	December 11	Ministry of Labour formed
	December 19	National Service instituted
	December 22	Ministries of Food, Pensions and Shipping set up
1917	*January 16*	General Lawson's Report recommends official employment of women with the Army in France
	February	Women's Land Army formed
	March 28	Army Council Instruction brings into being Women's Army Auxiliary Corps under Mrs Chalmers Watson
	April	10 women police appointed by the City of Liverpool
	June 25	First United States troops arrive in France

	August 21	Ministry of Reconstruction formed
	October	Board of Agriculture takes over sponsorship of Women's Institutes
	November 1	Katherine Furse resigns as Commandant of the VAD
	November 6	Battle of Paschendaele
	November 27	Dr Elsie Inglis dies on her return with SWH unit from Russia
	November 29	Women's Royal Naval Service (WRNS) set up under Katherine Furse
1918	January 2	Ministry of Air formed
	February 21	Department of Information becomes Ministry of Information
	February	Ministry of Labour appoints Commission of Enquiry into rumours of promiscuity among the WAAC
		National Council for the Unmarried Mother and Child founded
	April 1	Women's Royal Air Force set up, together with Royal Air Force
	April 10	National Service Act passed (to cover those of 50 years and over and service extended to Ireland)
	April 22	Hon. Violet Douglas-Pennant offered appointment as Commandant of WRAF
	May 19	German air raids on camps and hospitals at Etaples
	June 18	Miss Douglas-Pennant appointed Commandant of WRAF
	August 16	Miss Douglas-Pennant requests permission to resign appointment
	August 17	Permission to resign refused
	August 28	Miss Douglas-Pennant 'summarily dismissed' as Commandant
	November 11	Armistice
	December 1	British and US troops cross German frontier
	December 4	Army demobilisation begins
	December 6	Cologne entered by British forces
	December 11	General Election 1918: women over 30 given the vote

A note on the official photographers

Regrettably it has proved impossible to provide an attribution for every photograph in this book. More than twenty 'official' photographers worked for the British and Dominion governments, and in addition photographs were bought by the official agencies from private individuals, the press, and commercial photographic agencies such as the Topical Press, Alfieri, and Sport and General. The records of the Department of Information (DoI), and later the Ministry of Information (MoI), by whom most of the photographers were ultimately employed, are either incomplete or missing. Because of this it was decided that an attribution would be made only where the identity of the photographer was not in doubt. The extent of the information available varies considerably, and in some cases, consists of little more than a surname and an indication of where the individual worked. Information on Olive Edis, who was not an 'official' photographer, appears with her portrait in the main body of the text. The work of Horace W. Nicholls and G. P. Lewis, including many of the pictures which are reproduced here, was first shown to the public at an exhibition of Women's War Work which was held at Whitechapel Galleries, London in late 1918.

AITKEN, Thomas Keith

Born 1879. Worked before the war as a professional photographer on a Glasgow newspaper. Rejected as unfit for service in 1917, but in December of that year commissioned as an honorary Second Lieutenant and sent to France by the DoI, subsequently taken over by the MoI. Apart from two weeks on the Italian Front at the end of July 1918, worked on the Western Front. He was admitted to hospital at the beginning of August 1918, discharged and returned to work only to be gassed on 30 August. By September he was back at work, with the Canadian Corps, but was again admitted to hospital at the end of November 1918 at which juncture his career with the MoI appears to have ceased. Aitken used a Goertz 5 × 4 camera with a 4.5 lens.

LEWIS, G. P.

Described himself as 'over military age' in 1914. Worked as a professional photographer in the Far East before 1914, but returned home to try and find work of 'national importance'. From the surviving correspondence which he had with the MoI, Lewis seems to have been a self-sufficient character with a sanguine temperament and a good sense of humour. Employed by the MoI on a semi-official basis from 30 April 1918 to photograph military and military-industrial subjects in the United Kingdom. He worked through the summer of

1918, travelling the length and breadth of Britain on the Women's Work project for the Imperial War Museum, completing over a thousand photographs. Lewis, in common with most professional photographers at this period, seems to have used a half-plate camera with a 4.5 or 6.3 lens, although the make is not recorded.

NICHOLLS, Horace W.

A professional photographer with an established pre-war reputation through his famous series of 'Derby Day' photographs, and his work in South Africa during the Second Boer War 1899–1902. He applied, as early as September 1916, to work as an 'official' photographer but was not employed until June 1917 when the DoI took him on to take photographs for use in propaganda publications; this scheme was expanded three months later to permit the issue of these pictures to the press. During 1918 Nicholls was employed by the DoI and later the MoI, in conjunction with the Imperial War Museum to take photographs for the Museum's Women's Work project. He continued to work for the Museum following the closure of the MoI in December 1918. There are over two thousand examples of Nicholls's work in the Museum's collections. Other examples of his work can be found at the Royal Photographic Society.

APPENDIX 2
LIBRARIES AND ARCHIVES HOLDING MANUSCRIPT COLLECTIONS AND PHOTOGRAPHS

The Fawcett Library
City of London Polytechnic
Calcutta House
Old Castle Street
London E1 7NT

Papers of Josephine Butler, Maude Royden, Elizabeth Garrett Anderson, Eleanor Rathbone, Teresa Billington-Greig et al. The collections also include the papers of several women's organisations, together with photographs, posters and newspaper cuttings.

Imperial War Museum
Lambeth Road
London SE1 6HZ

Women's Work Collection administered by the Department of Printed Books. The collection was formed between 1917 and 1920 and covers virtually every aspect of women's work during the First World War. Private papers of several prominent women including the Diaries of Mairi Chisholm and material relating to Flora Sandes administered by the Department of Documents. Over 4,000 photographs covering women's work in industry and the voluntary and uniformed services administered by the Department of Photographs. The Department of Sound Records has an extensive collection of recordings covering work by women on the land, in munitions and in the Services, and the Department of Film holds a number of interesting early films of women in the First World War. The Department of Art has an extensive collection of posters as well as paintings and bronzes of and by women.

Public Record Office
Ruskin Avenue
Kew
Surrey

References to women's work can be found in virtually every obvious place, and in some of the less obvious. The main introduction to what is available can be established by consulting the papers of the government departments in which women were employed in large numbers. Thus the papers of the Ministry of Munitions, War Office and Ministry of Agriculture, Fisheries and Food are invaluable.

SELECT BIBLIOGRAPHY

This bibliography does not claim to be comprehensive, but is simply intended as an introduction and guide to the wealth of source material which is available.
All books published in London unless otherwise indicated.

Biography and memoirs

Bondfield, Margaret,	*A Life's Work* (Hutchinson, 1949).
Brittain, Vera,	*Testament of Youth* (Virago Press, 1978).
Clark-Kennedy, A. E.,	*Edith Cavell – Pioneer & Patriot* (Faber & Faber, 1965).
Cooper, Lady Diana,	*The Rainbow Comes and Goes* (Rupert Hart-Davis, 1958).
Dent, Olive,	*A V.A.D. in France* (Grant Richards, 1917).
Douglas-Pennant, V.,	*Under The Search-Light* (George Allen & Unwin, 1922).
Emslie Hutton, I.,	*With a Women's Unit in Serbia, Salonika and Sebastopol* (Williams & Norgate, 1928).
Farmborough, Florence,	*Nurse at the Russian Front – A Diary 1914–18* (Constable, 1974).
Furse, Katherine,	*Hearts & Pomegranates* (Peter Davies, 1940).
George, Gertrude A.,	*Eight Months with The Women's Royal Air Force* (Heath Granton, 1920).
Lawrence, Dorothy,	*Sapper Dorothy Lawrence* (John Lane – The Bodley Head, 1918).
Lloyd George, David,	*War Memoirs* (2 vols, Odhams, 1938).
Londonderry, Lady,	*Retrospect* (Frederick Muller, 1938).
Luard, K.,	*Unknown Warriors* (Chatto & Windus, 1930).
McDougal, G.,	*Nursing Adventures – A FANY in France* (William Heinemann, 1917).
Pope-Hennessy, James,	*Queen Mary* (George Allen & Unwin, 1959).
St Clair Stobart, Mrs,	*The Flaming Sword in Serbia and Elsewhere* (Hodder & Stoughton, 1927).
Sandes, Flora,	*The Autobiography of A Woman Soldier* (Witherby, 1927).
T'Serclaes, Baroness de,	*Flanders and Other Fields* (Harrap, 1964).

General histories

Adam-Smith, Patsy,   *Australian Women at War* (Nelson, Melbourne, 1984).

Braybon, Gail,   *Women Workers in The First World War: The British Experience* (Croom Helm, 1981).

Burk, Kathleen (ed.),   *War And The State: The Transformation of British Government 1914–1919* (George Allen & Unwin, 1982).

Cowper, Col. J. M.,   *A Short History of Queen Mary's Army Auxiliary Corps* (WRAC Association, Aldershot, 1966).

Crutwell, C. R. M. F.,   *A History of The Great War 1914–1918* (2nd ed., Oxford, 1936).

Kirkaldy, A. W. (ed.),   *British Labour-Replacement and Conciliation 1914–21* (Isaac Pitman, 1921).

Krippner, Monica,   *The Quality of Mercy – Women at War 1915–18* (David & Charles, 1980).

Lewis, Jane,   *Women In England 1870–1950: Sexual Divisions & Social Change* (Wheatsheaf Books, Sussex, 1984).

Lock, Joan,   *The British Policewoman – Her Story* (Robert Hale, 1979).

Marwick, Arthur,   *The Deluge – British Society and The First World War* (Macmillan, 1965).

Marwick, Arthur,   *Women at War 1914–1918* (Croom Helm, 1977).

Medlicott, W. N.,   *Contemporary England 1914–1964* (Longman, 1967).

Mitchell, David,   *Women on the Warpath* (Cape, 1966).

Munitions, Ministry of,   *History of The Ministry of Munitions Vol VI – Manpower & Dilution* (HMSO, 1922).

Pankhurst, E. Sylvia,   *The Suffragette Movement* (Longmans Green, 1931).

Pankhurst, E. Sylvia,   *The Home Front* (Hutchinson, 1932).

Raeburn, Antonia,   *The Militant Suffragettes* (Michael Joseph, 1973).

Rosen, Andrew,   *Rise Up, Women!* (Routledge & Kegan Paul, 1974).

Taylor, A. J. P.,   *English History 1914–1945* (Oxford University Press, 1965).

Tuchman, Barbara,   *The Proud Tower: A portrait of the world before the war 1890–1914* (Hamish Hamilton, 1966).

Vicinus, Martha,   *Independent Women – Work and Community For Single Women 1850–1920* (Virago Press, 1985).

Williams, Val,   *Women Photographers: The Other Observers 1900 to the Present* (Virago Press, 1986).

Wiltsher, Anne,   *Most Dangerous Women – Feminist Peace Campaigners of The Great War* (Pandora Press, 1985).

INDEX

Aberconway, Lord and Lady, 15
Aberdeen (Scotland), 168
Agriculture, Board of, 60, 148, 154,
    Women's Board of, 60
Airlie, Mabel Countess of, 144
Aitken, Thomas K., 193
Albania, 43, 47
Aldershot (Hampshire), 57
Alexandra, HM Queen, 12, Rose Day,
    12
Allen, Mary S., 67
Almeric Paget Military Massage Corps,
    15, masseuse, 15, Mr and Mrs
    Almeric Paget, 15
Amalgamated Association of Tramway
    and Vehicle Workers, 90
American Expeditionary Force (AEF),
    124
Anderson, Dr Elizabeth Garrett, 42,
    174
Anderson, Dr Louisa Garrett, 42, 45,
    51
Army Ordnance Department, 78
Army Service Corps (ASC), 88, 144,
    148
Australian Forces, 34

Baker, Dr Lily, 53
Balkan War, 34, 47
Barker, Miss Lilian, 105, 112
Barnes, Mrs Gerard, 169
(Messrs) Barry Ostlers & Shepherd Ltd,
    78
Beatrice, HRH The Princess, 12
Becher, Dame Ethel, 32
Belgian Army, 40, 46, 47
Belgian Relief Fund, 8
Belgium, places in: Aire, 27, Brussels,
    38–9, Doullens, 23, Pervyse, 40, 46,
    Ramscapelle, 40, Watten, 26
Berkshire, 89
Bigge, Miss, 114
Birmingham, 100, 163, 165
Blake, William, 1

Bondfield, Margaret, 22, 56, 71
Boyle, Miss Nina, 67
British Expeditionary Force (BEF), 30,
    116, 131
British Red Cross Society (BRCS), see
    Red Cross
Brittain, Vera, 22, 29
Brooke, Rupert, 22
Brunner Mond & Co, 87
Buckinghamshire, 96
Butcher, Miss M., 131

casualties, 38, children, 38, men, 38,
    women, 38, 60
Cavell, Edith, 22, 70, background, 38,
    nursing career in Brussels, 38,
    wartime activities, 39, trial and
    execution, 39
Central Committee for Women's
    Training and Employment, 9, 22, 71
Chalmers Watson, Mrs, 116, 131
Charles Mackintosh & Sons Ltd, 100
Chauncey, Miss, 53
Child labour, 9
Chilwell Factory (Nottingham), 105
Chisholm, Miss Mairi, 40, 46, 125
class, 2–9, 29, 115, middle, 2–9, 13–
    21, 59, 63, 115, upper, 2–9, 12–21,
    49, 59, 63, 115, working, 2–9, 15,
    63, 72, 79, 115
Clifton Power Station, 160
Clydeside (Scotland), 95
Commonwealth War Graves
    Commission, 180
Conway, Agnes, 128, 174, 182
Croix de Guerre (France), 70

Damer Dawson, Margaret, 67
death, attitudes to, 38, of men, 157,
    172, 180, 182, of women, 38, 43,
    113, 180, 182
Defence of the Realm Act, 1914
    (DORA), 23
domestic service, 7, 79, 90, 91

East London Federation, 56, 71
Edinburgh (Scotland), 42
Edis, Olive (Olive Edis Galsworthy), 128, 174, 182
Egger, 'Lady Major', 57
Emerson, Sister, 15

Fawcett, Millicent Garrett, 7, 56
Fire Brigade, 168
First Aid Nursing Yeomanry (FANY), 46, 49, 51, 70
food, coupon, 18, rationing, 18, shortages, 16–18
Forster, Mrs Rosanna, 10
France, places in, Abbéville, 30, 121, 128, 136, 180, Béthune, 30, Boulogne, 32, 50, Bourges, 124, Calais, 29, 46, 49, Dieppe, 116, Dunkirk, 19, Etaples, 25, 38, 182, Le Touquet, 19, Rouen, 28, 119, 120, 128, Wimereux, 45
franchise, 2
Fraser, Henriette Maud, 70
Frederick Tibbenham Ltd, 109
Fullerton, Colonel, 45
Furse, Charles W, 131
Furse, Dame Katherine (VADs and WRNS), 52, 131

Galsworthy, John, 174
Geddes, Sir Eric, 131
George V, HM King, 18
German, 30, 39, 136, 148
Girl Guides Association, 16, 59
Glasgow Battalion of WVR, 54
Glasgow Corporation, 99
Glasgow Gas Department, 83, 87
Glasgow Tramways Department, 90, 98, 165
Glebe Sugar Refinery, 86
Grantham (Lincs), 67
Graves Registration Service (later Commonwealth War Graves Commission), 180
Great Eastern Railway Co., 93
Great Western Railway Co., 91
Greenhalgh, Mrs Mabel Ann Stobart, see St Clair Stobart,
Greenock (Scotland), 86

Hamilton-Lawrence, Mrs, 70
Hare, Dr Dorothy (Asst. Medical Director WRNS), 52
Harland and Wolff Ltd, 95
Haslemere (Surrey), 15
Haverfield, The Hon Evelina, 55
Heathfield (Sussex), 142, 153, 172
Hebburn-on-Tyne (County Durham), 104, 175

Hospital, barges, 26–27, flying field, 47, Hilders Hospital (Haslemere), 15, Australian, 34, Duchess of Sutherland's, 29, Duchess of Westminster's, 19, 176, 4 Stationary, 30, 9 Canadian Stationary, 38, 25 Stationary, 28, 32 Stationary, 45, trains, 30, ships, 38, Women's Hospital, (see Women's Hospital Corps), 45

Imperial War Museum, 82, 128, 152, 174
income tax, 2, 6
Inglis, Dr Elsie Maud, background, 42, formation of Scottish Women's Hospitals, 22, 42, medical work abroad, 42, death, 42
Ipswich (Suffolk), 109

Jex-Blake, Dr Sophia, 42
Johnson, Amy, 138
Joseph Crossfield & Sons Ltd, 82

Kirkaldy (Scotland), 78
Knocker, Mrs Elsie, *see* T'Serclaes, Baroness de and Women of Pervyse

Labour Party, 2, 71
Lady Instructor's Signals Company, 57
Lady's Pictorial, May 1915, 8
Lancashire, 72, 79, 82, 100, 104, 160
League of Rights, 71
Légion d'Honneur (France), 70
Leslie, Dr R. Murray, 13
Lewis, G P, 9, 82, 104, 123, 193–4
Lloyd George, David, 62, 73
(Messrs) Loders & Mucoline Ltd, 87
Loftus, Susie, 95
London, Clapham, 96, Crystal Palace, 131, Euston, 64, Highbury, 61, Marylebone, 105, Paddington, 91, Park Royal, 112, Silvertown, 87, Woolwich, *see* Woolwich
London County Council, 105
London General Omnibus Company, 90, 100
London Underground, 93
Londonderry, Edith Marchioness of, 55, 63, 115
Lowestoft (Suffolk), 118, 125, 128
(Messrs) Lyle & Co, 163

Macarthur, Mary, 8–9, 22, 56, 71
McCarthy, Dame Maude, 32
Macdougal, Mrs G., 51
McGregor, Dr Beatrice, 43
Manners, Lady Diana, 22, 29

Mapstone Graham, Mrs, 14
Mary, HRH The Princess, 12, 75, 154
Mary, HM Queen, 8–9, 12, 18, 22, 69, 71, 144, 154
Mayfair Window Cleaning Company, 94, 156
Mechanical Transport Company (MTC) no. 814, 50
Metropolitan Police, 64, 66–7
Military Medal, 40, 180
Moore, Decima, 55
Mothers' Arms, The, 71
Munitions, Ministry of, 62, 68, 73, 105, 107
Murray, Dr Flora, 45, 51

National Federation of Women Workers (NFWW), 71
National Shell Filling Factories (NSFF), 105, 111
National Union of Women's Suffrage Societies (NUWSS), 3, 7, 8
National Union of Women Teachers (NUWT), 21
National Union of Women Workers (NUWW), 56, 60, 64–6
Newcastle (England), 42
Nicholls, Horace W, 10, 11, 20, 74, 142, 144, 145, 148, 152, 194
Nicholls, Miss, 128
Nightingale, Florence, 21, 25
No-Conscription Fellowship, 56
Norman, Lady Priscilla, 128, 182
North, Miss, 28
Nottingham (England), 79

Order of the British Empire, 131
Order of St John of Jerusalem, 13, 20, 131
Order of Karageorge (Serbia), 41
Order of Leopold (Belgium), 40
Order of the Red Cross (Serbia), 43
Order of St Sava (Serbia), 43
Osea Island (Essex), 113, 132

Paget, Mr and Mrs Almeric, *see* Almeric Paget Massage Corps
Paget, Leila, Lady, 47
Palmers Shipbuilding Yard, 104, 175
Pankhurst, Christobel, 2, 56, 71
Pankhurst, Emmeline, 2, 56, 62, 71, 73, 174
Pankhurst (Estelle) Sylvia, 2, 56, 71
Pares, Miss, 43
Park Royal Munitions Factory, 112
part-time employment, 61, 64, 66
Patterson, Dr, 28

Pavlova Leather Company, 89
pay, 9, 30, 53, 60, 71, 98, 99, 111, 116
Pershing, General, 124
Pethick-Lawrence, Mrs, 55
poison gas, 125
Police, see Metropolitan and women police
Post Office, 92
Prince of Wales, HRH The, 29
Princess Mary's Soldiers' and Sailors' Christmas Fund, 75
Princess Victoria Rest Club for Nurses, 25

Queen Alexandra's Imperial Military Nursing Service (QAIMNS), 26–7, 32
Queen Mary's Army Auxiliary Corps (QMAAC), *see* WAAC
Queen Mary's Needlework Guild, 12
Queen's Work For Women Fund, 9, 71

(Messrs) Rank & Sons, 82
Red Cross, 19–53, 49, British Red Cross Society (BRCS), 9, 13, 131, Serbian Red Cross, 41
Reform Act, 1911, 2
Richard Williams, Drapers (Clapham), 96
Royal Air Force, 136
Royal Army Medical Corps (RAMC), 27, 53
Royal Flying Corps, 136, 140
Royal Marines, 117
Royal Naval Air Service, 136
Royal Navy, 42, 118, 123, 131
Russian Revolution, 42

St Clair Stobart, Mrs (Mabel Ann Stobart Greenhalgh), background, 47, Bulgian war work, 47, Belgarian war work, 47, Serbian War work, 47
St John of Jerusalem, Order of, *see* Order of
Salonika (Greece), 41
Sandes, Flora, 41
schoolgirls, 16
Scoones, Miss, 15
Scottish Suffrage Societies, 42
Scottish Women's First Aid Corps, 14
Scottish Women's Hospitals (SWH), 22, 42
Serbia, places in, 4, 41, 42, Belgrade, 41, Kragujerac, 42, 43, Mladenovac, 43, Sarajevo, 4

Serbian Relief Fund, 8, 47
Shell shortage, 62, 73
Signallers' Corps (WVR), 59
Smith, Edith, 67
Soltau, Dr G. Eleanor, 43
South East & Chatham Railway
  Company, 88, 96, 171
South Metropolitan Gas Company, 104
Sparsholt, Miss, 61
Stanley, Mrs Theo, 66
Starr, Miss, 124
(Messrs) Stewart & Co., 168
Substitution, 10, 74, 86, 94
Suffragettes, 3–4, 55, 56, 57, 62, 69
Suffragists, 3–4, 47, 56, 69, 70
Sutherland, Duchess of, 29, 55
Swansea (Wales), 182
sweated trades, 7–9

Tarrant Huts, 104
Territorial Force Nursing Service
  (TFNS), 26–7, 33
Textile Industry, 3–7, 73, 79
Thetford (Norfolk), 10
(Messrs) Thew, Hooker Silby Ltd, 89
Trade Unions, 2–7, 55, 62, 73, 88
Trades Union Congress (TUC), 71
TNT (Trinitrotoluene), 87, 105
T'Serclaes, Baroness de (Elsie Knocker),
  40, 125
Turner Brothers Asbestos Factory, 104

Uxbridge (Middlesex), 148–51

Vickers Ltd, 110
Victoria, HM Queen, 1, Victorian, 3,
  15, 22, 26, 157
Voluntary Aid Detachments (VAD),
  20–38, 131, cooks, drivers, 50, 52,
  nurses, 20–38, 52, 68
Voluntary Women's Patrols, *see*
  Women Police
Vote, the, 3, 172
Votes For Women (suffrage periodical),
  70

Wade, Miss F, 119
Walthall, Miss, 61
War Office, 7, 21, 53
Welfare, medical, 60, 73, 105, moral,
  65, social, 9, 67, 69, Welfare
  Department (Min. of Munitions), 68
Westminster, Constance, Duchess of,
  19, 176
Wigan Coal and Iron Company Ltd, 72
Women, as: asbestos workers, 104,
  bakers, 116, billposters, 10,
  blacksmiths, 8, 51, booking clerks,

91, bus conductress, 90, cabinet
  minister, 71, carpenters, 104,
  cleaners, 54, 91, 158–60, chimney
  sweeps, 8, 10, coal workers, 72–3,
  cooks, 116, 120, drivers, 40, 46, 49,
  50, 136, 140, 165, funeral hearse
  drivers, 11, gravediggers, 11, grave
  tenders, 180, 182, inspectors
  (agricultural), 60, medical officers,
  45, 51, 52, munitionettes, 68, 105–
  13, 175, 182, office workers, 91,
  116, 124, postwomen, 92, printers,
  116, 121, railway workers, 88, 91,
  93, 96, 158–60, 165, 171, rubber
  factory workers, 100, shipyard
  workers, 87, 104, stewards (air raid
  shelters), 61, telegraph and
  telephone operators, 91, 116, ticket
  collectors, 91, vehicle fitters, 100,
  window cleaners, 94, 156
Women's Army Auxiliary Corps
  (WAAC) (later Queen Mary's Army
  Auxiliary Corps), 10, 110, 116, 120,
  124, 128, 131, 136, 140, 176, 180,
  182
Women's Auxiliary Force (WAF), 61
Women's Emergency Corps (WEC), 8,
  9, 22, 40, 54, 55, 57
Women's Emergency League (WEL),
  57
Women's Farm and Garden Union, 154
Women's Forage Corps (WFC), 60, 148
Women's Forestry Corps (WFC), 60,
  142, 152, 172
Women's Freedom League (WFL)
Women's Hospital Corps, 22, in France,
  45, 51, in Endell Street London, 51
Women's Land Army (WLA), 60, 148
Women's Legion, 55, 115, 136, 140,
  agricultural section, 63, canteen
  section, 63, military cookery section,
  63
women's movement, 3
Women's National Land Service Corps,
  154
Women of Pervyse, 22, 40, *see also*
  Mairi Chisholm and T'Serclaes,
  Baroness de
Women Police, 55–6, 64–7
Women's Right to Serve March 1915,
  62
Woman's Royal Naval Service (WRNS),
  52, 117, 118, 123, 125, 131–33,
  169
Women's Royal Air Force (WRAF), 53,
  136, 138, 141
Women's Sick and Wounded Convoy
  Corps, 47

Women's Social and Political Union, 2, 3, 56, 71

Women's Trades Union League, 8

Women's Training and Employment, Central Committee For, *see* Central Committee

Women's Transport Service, *see* FANY

Women's Volunteer Reserve (WVR), 54, 55, 57, 59, 63

Woolwich (London), Arsenal, 105, Babies' Home, 69

Workers' Suffrage Federation, 56

Zeppelin, 38